The Spear and the Spindle

Ancestors of Sir Frances Bryan (d. 1550), Kt.,

Chief Gentleman of the Privy Chamber
for Henry VIII of England;

Bryan, Bourchier, Bohun, FitzAlan,
and others;

Including Kings and Queens
of England, France, and Other Countries;
Some Magna Carta Sureties,

and Some Descendants,
Including Those Commonly Believed
to be Ancestors of
Rebecca Bryan (m. Daniel Boone)

T. A. Fuller

D1072896

HERITAGE BOOKS
2008

HERITAGE BOOKS
AN IMPRINT OF HERITAGE BOOKS, INC.

Books, CDs, and more—Worldwide

For our listing of thousands of titles see our website
at
www.HeritageBooks.com

Published 2008 by
HERITAGE BOOKS, INC.
Publishing Division
100 Railroad Ave. #104
Westminster, Maryland 21157

International Standard Book Numbers
Paperbound: 978-1-55613-842-3
Clothbound: 978-0-7884-7136-0

The Spear and the Spindle:
Ancestors of Sir Francis Bryan (d. 1550)
Bryan, Bourchier, Bohun, FitzAlan, and Others

Contents

The Spear and the Spindle:
Ancestors of Sir Francis Bryan (d. 1550)
Bryan, Bourchier, Bohun, FitzAlan, and Others

Contents

The Spear and the Spindle:
Ancestors of Sir Francis Bryan (d. 1550)
Bryan, Bourchier, Bohun, FitzAlan, and Others

Foreword

"The spear half" and "the spindle half" are words used in King Alfred's will* to designate the male and female parts of his family. Alfred the Great was King of England 871-901 and is considered one of the greatest men in history. He is an ancestor of Sir Francis Bryan and many of the people in this manuscript.

None of the information in this manuscript has been gathered firsthand. Rather, it has been taken from others who have taken it firsthand (as in *The Complete Peerage*) or it may have been obtained as far along as fourth hand. And it has been gathered from many sources (see **Bibliography and References**). The key word is *gathered*. This manuscript is a compilation.

The difficult part has been in focus. While it takes only two people to make one descendant, it took four to make those two, and eight to make those four—and, as every genealogist knows, it is easy to lose sight of where you are, where you are heading, and where you need to go. In an effort to narrow the focus, the number of people in this manuscript has been limited to twelve generations of ancestors of Sir Francis Bryan.

Sir Francis Bryan was descended from Edward III, and thus, of course, from preceding kings and queens of England, France, and other countries, from William I the Conqueror, and from Charlemagne. And, if this compiled information is correct, he was descended from at least eleven Sureties for the Magna Charta. Surety Roger Bigod (RIN 202) is not listed on this table due to the generation limit, but his son Hugh de Bigod (RIN 177) is included here and was also a Surety for the Magna Charta. Robert de Vere, the father of Hugh de Vere (RIN 133), was a Surety. Sir Francis Bryan was also descended from Robert de Roos (d. 1226) and William Malet (d. abt 1217), neither of which appear on this limited generation table.

Bryan's mother, Margaret Bourchier, was half-sister of Queen Anne Boleyn's mother and was the "Lady Bryan" so often mentioned in histories as being entrusted with the care of Henry VIII's children, Mary and Elizabeth. The two princesses would become the English queens known as "Bloody Mary" and Elizabeth the Great.

---

* Besant, Walter, *Story of King Alfred*, D. Appleton and Company, 1902, pg. 183.

The Spear and the Spindle:
Ancestors of Sir Francis Bryan (d. 1550)
Bryan, Bourchier, Bohun, FitzAlan, and Others

Foreword

There are holes in this pedigree. That is disappointing, but it is exciting because of the future possibilities they bring. If the reader can fill in any of the holes, your compiler and other readers would appreciate your information. It could tie us in to many more interesting families. Please include your references or sources.

The **Bibliography and References** section is not limited to the books mentioned in this manuscript. It is a broader listing of materials which may prove valuable to you in your own research.

Use the **Bibliography and References** also as a pleasure reading list. The books by Plaidy (her name is actually Eleanor Hibbert, b. 1906) are classified as historical fiction. However, her novels are quite suitable for those readers who are interested in the politics, motivations, and interrelationships of figures of medieval England. The advantage of reading history in novel form is that it is more entertaining and facts and relationships are more easily retained by the reader. Her work is well researched and pleasantly accurate as well as pleasantly read.

One of the sources for this manuscript, *Ancestral Roots of Sixty Colonists Who Came to New England between 1623 and 1650* by Frederick Lewis Weis, is especially valuable because Weis lists several sources for his information, whereas your compiler is listing only him. By checking out the Weis book, you are coming into other sources and a wealth of other related genealogical information. The work of Weis (b. 22 Aug 1895, d. 11 Apr 1966) has been continued in editions incorporating corrections and new material, an effort that has been carefully coordinated by Walter Lee Sheppard, Jr.

The Magna Charta by Wurts is referenced and referred to in the text biographies. *The Magna Charta* can be an invaluable guide. Some genealogists complain of errors in Wurts, but the careful researcher always compares information from different sources, and errors in any source are made evident.

If your public or university library or your bookseller does not have the books you need, tell your librarian you would like to request an interlibrary loan. The books will be borrowed from another library and delivered to your local library. Libraries are always glad to be of assistance to responsible borrowers.

People often question the validity of these old lines. However, the information concerning the old genealogy may be more reliable than

Foreword

The Spear and the Spindle:
Ancestors of Sir Francis Bryan (d. 1550)
Bryan, Bourchier, Bohun, FitzAlan, and Others

many of our documents of recent days. Over the centuries, scholars and historians have combed the old documents and translated, discussed, and verified the information innumerable times. There is a wealth of information from different sources on this time period, and new information is always coming to light.

Source notations have been included as assiduously as possible; however, there is so much material that some references may have been inadvertently omitted. Where your compiler has been certain of the information, it has been included rather than withdrawn. As with any reference source, the reader is requested to treat this manuscript as a guide for his own research.

Some individuals are referenced with Record Identification Numbers (RINs), yet they do not appear in this manuscript. Those persons appear elsewhere in the genealogical database but may not be known at this time to be part of this 13-generation table. Their RINs are included because your compiler hopes to produce other **Spear and Spindle** publications that may contain some of the individuals on this family tree. RINs from publication to publication will be constant for each individual and assist in the identification of ancestors.

The computer printout program may have truncated the name of some individuals in the thirteenth generation due to limited chart space. An effort has been made to list those names in full in the **Short Biographies** section, either under the name of the individual or under the name of the issue. Occasionally a truncation may result in a single *T*, a truncation of *The Surety* in your compiler's computer database. Again, an effort has been made to clarify such pertinent information in the **Short Biographies** section.

An individual's location on the charts of the genealogical table can be found in the **Index of Names on Table**. That individual might also be found in the **Short Biographies** section that follows the table. There, individuals are listed alphabetically by name and further identified by RIN and death dates when known. A second section of short biographies contains some interesting collaterals and further genealogical information.

This material was compiled with the aid of the computer genealogy program PAF — Personal Ancestral File, which is obtained from the Church of Latter Day Saints. PAF keeps track of all relationships and prints various ancestry charts. It assigns each person an RIN and an

The Spear and the Spindle:
Ancestors of Sir Francis Bryan (d. 1550)
Bryan, Bourchier, Bohun, FitzAlan, and Others   **Foreword**

MRIN (Marriage Record Identification Number). These RINs are most helpful, especially if your ancestors have insisted on using the same name. A good genealogy program is an invaluable aid for keeping your spears and spindles in order.

The Spear and the Spindle:
Ancestors of Sir Francis Bryan (d. 1550)
Bryan, Bourchier, Bohun, FitzAlan, and Others

How to Use the Index of Names

Names included on the genealogical table are listed alphabetically in the "Index of Names on Table." Note the column headings.

Column Headings of Index

- "RIN" indicates a person's Record Identification Number. The RIN remains constant throughout the table and biographies.

- "Born/Chr" indicates the year of birth or christening when known.

- "Died/Bur" indicates the year of death or burial when known.

- "Chart Number" indicates which pedigree chart holds the first appearance of that person in the charts. (The person may also appear on other charts.)

- "Person Number" indicates the location on the chart where the person is printed.

- "Parent MRIN" indicates the Marriage Record Identification Number of the couple (married or not).

The Spear and the Spindle
Ancestors of Sir Francis Bryan (d. 1550)
Bryan, Bourchier, Bohun, FitzAlan, and Others   How to Use the Index of Names

The Spear and the Spindle:
Ancestors of Sir Francis Bryan (d. 1550)
Bryan, Bourchier, Bohun, FitzAlan, and Others

How to Read the Charts of the Table

Chart No. 1

There are many
charts to this table.
This is Chart No. 1

16 Thomas BRYAN-1650--------

8 Edm ----

B:

P:

M: --969

Individual is
continued on
this chart no.

17

Birth
Place
Married
Place
Died
Place

4 Sir Thomas BRYAN-1631-------------

B:

P:

M: --960

P:

D: 1500

P:

D:

P:

18 S BURES-1649-------------

9 Alice BURES-1648----------------

B:

19 -------------------

P:

D:

P:

20 -------------------

2 Sir Thomas BRYAN-1625-------------

B:

P:

M: --956

P:

D:

P:

Individual's
position
on this chart

10 Sir John BOWSEY-1644------------

B:

P:

M: --967

P:

D:

P:

21 -------------------

5 Margaret BOWSEY-1643--------------

B:

P:

D:

P:

22 Richard BARNES-1646------

11 Margaret BARNES-1645------------

B:

23 -------------------

P:

D:

P:

RIN —
individual's
Record
Identification
Number

24 S BOURCHIER-1614---------

1 Sir Francis BRYAN-1626------------

B: 1490

P:

M: Aft 1517 --957

P:

D: 2 Feb 1550/1551

P: Clonmel,Ireland

Philippa MONTGOMERY-1627-------

Spouse

12 Sir John BOURCHIER-1617----------

B:

P: 1st Lord Berners

M: --952

P:

D: May 1474

P:

3

25 Anne PLANTAGENET-1613----

4

6 Sir Humphrey BOURCHIER-1619-------

B:

P:

M: --953

P:

D: 14 Apr 1471

P: Battle of B

MRIN —
their
Marriage
Record
Number

26 S BERNERS-1628-----------

13 Margery BERNERS-1618------------

B:

P:

D: 18 Dec 1475

P:

27 P DALYNGRIDGE-1629-------

5

28 -------------------

3 Margaret L BOURCHIER-1624---------

B:

P:

D: 1551/1552

P:

14 Sir Frederick TYLNEY-1621--------

B:

P:

M: --954

P:

D:

P:

29 -------------------

30 L CHENEY, ESQ.-1623------

7 Elizabeth TYLNEY-1620-------------

B:

P:

D: 4 Apr 1497

P:

15 Elizabeth CHENEY-1622-----------

B:

P:

D:

P:

31 -------------------

The Spear and the Spindle:
Ancestors of Sir Francis Bryan (d. 1550)
Bryan, Bourchier, Bohun, FitzAlan, and Others

How to Read the Quick Reference Tables

The entries of some individuals in the Short Biographies section are illustrated with quick reference tables. The tables contain three generations.

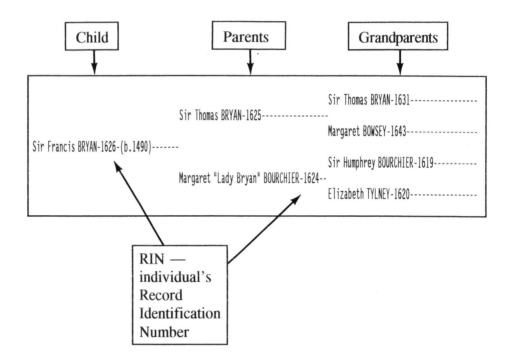

The Spear and the Spindle:
Ancestors of Sir Francis Bryan (d. 1550)
Bryan, Bourchier, Bohun, FitzAlan, and Others

Index of Names on Table

Name	RIN	Born/ Chr	Died/ Bur	Chart Number	Person Number	Parent MRIN
,Annora	1721			23	31	
,Emma	1641			3	17	
,Juliane	1718			23	13	
ADELAIDE,of Guelders	1672	1186	1218	16	13	983
ADELAIDE,of Holland	582	1225	1284	16	3	980
ADELAIDE/ALIX	1736			16	19	
AENOR	1609		1130	12	19	780
AGNES	1763			17	11	1038
AGNES,of Blois	1744	1138	1207	17	25	
AGNES,of Hainault	1748	1142	1168	17	31	325
ALBERIC I	664	1110	1183	13	24	558
ALBERIC II	662	1135	1200	13	12	361
ALFONSO II,King of Aragon	639	1152	1196	12	24	856
ALFONSO II,King of Provence	637	1180	1209	8	20	347
ALFONSO IX,King of Leon	649	1166	1229	13	4	353
ALICE,of France	1034	1170	1218	13	15	344
ALIX/ADELA/ALICE,of Champagne	634	1140	1206	13	31	778
ALPHONSO I,King of Portugal	1044			13	18	
ALPHONSO VII,King of Leon	1038	1103	1157	13	16	602
ALPHONSO VIII,King of Castile	1041	1155	1214	8	26	599
ANDREW II,King of Hungary	1591	1176	1235	14	14	940
ANGELINA,Anna	1765		1212	19	27	
ANNE/AGNES,of Chatillon	1594	1153	1184	14	29	990
ARCHAMBAUD IX,de Bourbon	665		1242	15	10	1022
ARCHAMBAUD V,de Montlucon	1728			15	22	
ARNSTEIN,Agnes von	625			17	23	
BADLESMERE,Bartholomew	103	1275	1322	4	26	304
BADLESMERE,Elizabeth	99	1313	1355	4	13	56
BADLESMERE,Guncelin/ Gunselm	556			22	2	
BALDWIN V,of Hainault	597	1150	1195	16	20	325
BALDWIN VI,of Hainaut	595	1171	1205	16	10	324
BARNES,Margaret	1645			1	11	968
BARNES,Richard	1646			1	22	
BEATRICE,de Montlucon	1727			15	11	1021
BEATRICE,of Savoy	636	1198	1266	8	11	348
BEATRICE,of St. Pol	1036	1160		13	29	595
BEATRIX,of Provence	1677	1234	1267	19	5	345
BEATRIX,of Vienne	644		1230	12	29	
BEAUCHAMP,Isabel	124		1306	9	3	67
BEAUCHAMP,Walcheline de	233			9	24	129
BEAUCHAMP,William de	123	1237	1298	9	6	127
BEAUCHAMP,William de	231		1268	9	12	128
BELA III,King of Hungary	1593	1148	1196	14	28	941
BELA IV,King of Hungary	1588	1206	1270	19	12	939
BELLOMONT,Margaret	130		1234	7	27	71

The Spear and the Spindle:
Ancestors of Sir Francis Bryan (d. 1550)
Bryan, Bourchier, Bohun, FitzAlan, and Others   Index of Names on Table

Name	RIN	Born/ Chr	Died/ Bur	Chart Number	Person Number	Parent MRIN
BERENGARIA, of Barcelona	1040	1116	1148	13	17	601
BERENGARIA, of Castile	650		1244	13	5	598
BERINGERUS, Margaret	628	1221	1295	14	5	345
BERINGERUS, Raymund IV	635	1198	1245	8	10	346
BERKELEY, Maurice	1176	1271	1326	11	2	678
BERKELEY, Maurice de	1712	1218	1281	11	8	
BERKELEY, Milicent de (Ela)	1662		1322	2	29	677
BERKELEY, Thomas	1178		1321	11	4	1010
BERMINGHAM, Eve de	1720		1226	23	25	
BERNERS, Margery	1618		1475	1	13	958
BERNERS, Sir Richard	1628			1	26	
BIGOD, Hugh THE SURETY	177		1225	9	30	110
BIGOD, Isabel	176		1230	9	15	96
BLANCHE, of Artois	127	1248	1302	8	3	69
BLANCHE, of Castile	630	1188	1252	8	13	598
BLANCHE, of Navarre	1566	1180	1229	15	9	927
BLANCHE, of Navarre	735		1158	13	21	867
BOHUN IX, Humphrey	1615		1372	4	6	53
BOHUN V, Humphrey de	245	1208	1275	20	8	135
BOHUN VI, Humphrey de	241		1265	20	4	134
BOHUN VII, Humphrey de	239	1249	1298	20	2	132
BOHUN VIII, Humphrey de	100	1276	1321	4	24	131
BOHUN, Alianore/Eleanor	1612		1399	4	3	951
BOHUN, Henry de THE SURETY	247	1176	1220	20	16	136
BOHUN, William	98	1310	1360	4	12	54
BOLEBEC, Isabel de	138		1245	7	25	77
BOTILLER, Maud le	156		1283	6	9	89
BOTILLER, Theobald le	165			6	18	511
BOURBON, Marguerite de	1565	1211	1256	15	5	1020
BOURCHIER, Margaret L	1624		1551	1	3	953
BOURCHIER, Robert	1634		1349	3	4	963
BOURCHIER, Sir Humphrey	1619		1471	1	6	952
BOURCHIER, Sir John	1617		1474	1	12	950
BOURCHIER, Sir William	1632		1365	3	2	962
BOURCHIER, Sir William	1614		1420	1	24	961
BOWSEY, Margaret	1643			1	5	967
BOWSEY, Sir John	1644			1	10	
BRAOS, Alianore de	242			20	5	125
BRAOS, Eva	1187		1255	11	15	125
BRAOS, Reginald de	620		1227	20	20	443
BRIOUZE, Maud de	227		1300	6	11	125
BRIOUZE/BRAOS, William de	228			6	22	338
BRIWERE, Gracia de	621		1215	20	21	
BRUN, Alice/Alix le	120			7	5	81
BRUN, Hugh le	150			7	10	821
BRYAN, Edmund	1647			1	8	971

The Spear and the Spindle:
Ancestors of Sir Francis Bryan (d. 1550)
Bryan, Bourchier, Bohun, FitzAlan, and Others

Name	RIN	Born/ Chr	Died/ Bur	Chart Number	Person Number	Parent MRIN
BRYAN,Sir Francis	1626	1490	1550	1	1	956
BRYAN,Sir Thomas	1631		1500	1	4	969
BRYAN,Sir Thomas	1625			1	2	960
BRYAN,Sir William de	1652		1413	2	2	
BRYAN,Thomas	1650		1444	1	16	972
BURCER,John de	1636		1328	3	8	965
BURES,Alice	1648			1	9	970
BURES,Sir Robert de	1649			1	18	
BURSER,Robert de	1640			3	16	
CANTILUPE,Milicent de	1181			11	7	682
CANTILUPE,William de	1186		1254	11	14	1014
CANTILUPE,William de	1716			11	28	
CHARLES I,King of Naples a	1676	1220	1285	19	4	342
CHARLES II,King of Naples	1585	1248	1309	19	2	986
CHARLES,Count of Valois	1583	1270	1325	4	22	314
CHAWORTH,Maud	109		1322	2	27	60
CHAWORTH,Patrick de	583			9	4	
CHAWORTH,Sir Patrick de	110		1282	9	2	316
CHENEY, ESQ.,Lawrence	1623			1	30	
CHENEY,Elizabeth	1622			1	15	955
CLARE,Aveline de	619			9	29	207
CLARE,Gilbert de THE SURETY	367		1230	23	8	203
CLARE,Isabel de	180	1173	1220	7	19	102
CLARE,Margaret de	244		1333	4	27	182
CLARE,Maud de	359			23	21	203
CLARE,Richard de	324	1222	1262	23	4	206
CLARE,Richard de THE SURETY	362		1217	23	16	207
CLARE,Thomas de	322		1286	23	2	183
CLEMENCE,of Bar-le-Duc	1774		1183	13	27	
COLCHESTER,Helen de	1637		1249	3	9	964
COLCHESTER,Walter de	1638			3	18	
COURCI,Yolande de	1394	1168	1222	17	15	1031
COURTENAY,Yolande de	1724	1194	1233	14	15	116
D' AVESNES,William III	94	1286	1337	4	10	313
D'AUBIGNY,Isabel	158			6	17	86
D'AVESNES,Bouchard	593	1180	1221	16	4	1023
D'AVESNES,Jacques	1731	1150	1191	16	8	1024
D'AVESNES,John I	581	1218	1255	16	2	322
D'AVESNES,John II	575	1247	1304	4	20	315
D'AVESNES,Nicholas	1733		1169	16	16	
D'EU,Alice	254	1246	1246	20	19	500
DA. OF JACQUES	657			20	7	133
DALYNGRIDGE,Philippa	1629			1	27	959
DALYNGRIDGE,Sir Edward	1630			5	2	
DAMMARTIN,Agnes de	661			20	13	360
DAMMARTIN,Joanna	96	1208	1278	13	3	591

The Spear and the Spindle:
Ancestors of Sir Francis Bryan (d. 1550)
Bryan, Bourchier, Bohun, FitzAlan, and Others   Index of Names on Table

Name	RIN	Born/ Chr	Died/ Bur	Chart Number	Person Number	Parent MRIN
DAMMARTIN,Simon de C	1031	1180	1239	13	6	360
DE ESSEX,Anne	1656			3	11	
DHU,Gladys (Dark Eyes)	704		1215	6	21	387
DREUX,Philippa de	1740	1192	1242	17	7	823
ECHYNGHAM,Margaret	1651			1	17	
EDMUND,"Crouchback"	126	1244	1296	8	2	48
EDWARD I,King of England	89	1239	1307	4	16	48
EDWARD II,King of England	87	1284	1327	4	8	47
EDWARD III,King of England	85	1312	1377	4	4	46
ELEANOR,of Aquitaine	205	1122	1204	8	17	115
ELEANOR,of Castile	90	1244	1290	4	17	51
ELEANOR,of England	1042	1162	1214	8	27	111
ELEANOR,of Lancaster	105		1372	2	13	59
ELEANOR,of Provence	92	1217	1291	8	5	345
ELIZABETH	1201			12	23	690
ELIZABETH,of Kumans	1587		1290	19	7	987
ERMENSINDE,of Bar-sur-Seine	1742		1211	17	13	1029
ERMESINDE,of Luxemburg	1760	1075	1143	17	21	
ERMESINDE,of Namur	1750	1186	1247	17	5	1035
EUDOXIA	1693	1162	1202	14	27	999
FERDINAND III	95	1191	1252	13	2	352
FERNANDO II,King of Leon	651	1137	1188	13	8	597
FERRERS,Joan	1179		1309	11	5	332
FERRERS,William de	469	1193	1254	11	10	261
FERRIERES,William de	471		1247	11	20	262
FIENES,Ingelram de	659			20	6	359
FIENES,William de	660		1241	20	12	
FIENNES,Maud de	240			20	3	358
FITZALAN,Edmund	59	1285	1326	2	24	55
FITZALAN,Joan	1616			4	7	57
FITZALAN,Joan	1653		1404	2	3	973
FITZALAN,John I	157		1240	6	16	488
FITZALAN,John II	155		1267	6	8	85
FITZALAN,John III	115	1246	1271	6	4	84
FITZALAN,Richard I	111	1266	1301	6	2	63
FITZALAN,Richard II	104	1313	1375	2	12	31
FITZALAN,Sir John	1654		1379	2	6	57
FITZBERNARD,Joan	557			22	3	487
FITZBERNARD,Ralph	870			22	6	
FITZGEOFFREY,FitzJohn Maud	125		1301	9	7	95
FITZGEOFFREY,John FitzPiers	175		1258	9	14	337
FITZGEOFFREY,Maud	248		1236	20	17	137
FITZGERALD,Maurice	1717	1190	1257	23	12	1015
FITZMAURICE,Gerald	1719	1150	1203	23	24	
FITZMAURICE,Julian	323			23	3	184
FITZMAURICE,Sir Maurice	326		1286	23	6	996

The Spear and the Spindle:
Ancestors of Sir Francis Bryan (d. 1550)
Bryan, Bourchier, Bohun, FitzAlan, and Others

Name	RIN	Born/ Chr	Died/ Bur	Chart Number	Person Number	Parent MRIN
FITZPATRICK,Ela	699		1261	23	29	384
FITZPIERS,Geoffrey	251		1212	9	28	336
FITZROY,Isabel	1711		1276	11	9	1011
FITZROY,Richard	1713			11	18	1013
FLORENT III,Count of Holland	1670	1138	1190	16	24	
FLORENT IV,Count of Holland	1667	1210	1234	16	6	982
GEORGE,of Ceva/Cave	1710			6	14	
GERSENDA II,of Saban	638		1222	8	21	1019
GERSINDE	1726			12	27	
GERTRUDE,of Meran	1592		1213	19	25	989
GODFREY III,Count of Louvain	1704	1142	1186	16	28	1005
GODFREY,C. of Dagsburg	1759	1067	1139	17	20	1037
GORGES,Eleanor de	1665			10	3	
GUI	1745		1145	17	26	
GUI II,de Bourbon	1729		1216	15	20	
GUISE,Adele de	1732	1155		16	9	1025
GUISE,Bernard de	1735			16	18	
GWENTHLIN,Welthiana/	1661		1375	2	15	
HELEN,of Galloway	80			11	23	781
HENRY I,C. of Champagne	1675	1126	1181	15	16	
HENRY I,C. of Guelders	1764	1117	1182	17	22	
HENRY I,Duke of Brabant	1574	1165	1235	8	28	1004
HENRY I,King of Navarre	1444	1244	1274	15	2	925
HENRY II,Count of Bar	1739	1190	1239	17	6	1027
HENRY II,Duke of Brabant	1510	1207	1247	8	14	930
HENRY II,Duke of Limburg	1753	1110	1167	17	16	
HENRY II,King of England	204	1133	1189	8	16	112
HENRY III,Duke of Limburg	1751	1140	1221	17	8	1032
HENRY III,King of England	91	1206	1272	8	4	82
HENRY III,of Luxembourg	1666	1217	1281	17	2	590
HENRY,C. of Luxemburg	1758			17	10	1036
HENRY,of Lancaster	108	1281	1345	2	26	68
HUGH IX,de Lusignan	1389			7	20	
HUMBERT III,Count of Savoy	643		1188	12	28	418
HUNTINGDON,Ada de	1669	1146	1205	16	25	335
IRENE ANGELA	1512	1181	1208	8	31	886
ISABEL,of Angouleme Taillefer	151	1186	1246	7	11	339
ISABELLA,of Aragon	580	1243	1270	14	3	406
ISABELLA,of France	88	1292	1358	4	9	49
ISABELLA,of Hainault	632	1170	1189	8	25	324
JACQUES,Seigneur de	658			20	14	
JAMES I,King of Aragon	736	1207	1276	14	6	997
JEAN I,Count of Ponthieu	1035	1140	1191	13	28	594
JEANE,of Valois	577	1294	1342	4	11	934
JEANNE,de Navarre	578	1271	1304	4	19	851
JOHN,King of England	152	1166	1216	8	8	111

The Spear and the Spindle:
Ancestors of Sir Francis Bryan (d. 1550)
Bryan, Bourchier, Bohun, FitzAlan, and Others   Index of Names on Table

Name	RIN	Born/ Chr	Died/ Bur	Chart Number	Person Number	Parent MRIN
JOIGNY,Alix de (Courtenay)	623	1160	1205	7	23	689
KEVELIOC,Agnes of Chester	472		1247	11	21	88
KEVELIOK,Hawise	460		1242	23	23	88
KUTHEN/ZAYHAN,Prince	1678			19	14	
LACIE,John de THE SURETY	356		1240	23	10	201
LACIE,Maud de	325		1288	23	5	200
LACIE,Roger de	358		1211	23	20	202
LASCARIS I,Emperor Theodore	1590	1173	1222	19	26	1039
LASKARINA,Maria	1589	1206	1270	19	13	938
LIMBURG,Margaret von	1737	1139	1172	16	29	
LONGESPEE,Emmeline de	1690	1250	1291	23	7	118
LONGESPEE,Stephen	215		1274	23	14	382
LONGESPEE,William	698	1176	1225	23	28	383
LORETTE	230			7	15	
LOUIS IX,King of France	255	1214	1270	14	4	342
LOUIS VII,King of France	633	1119	1180	13	30	423
LOUIS VIII,King of France	629	1187	1226	8	12	343
LOUVAIN,Eleanor de	1633			3	3	966
LOUVAIN,Sir John de	1642			3	6	
LUISA,of Ceva/Cave	118			6	7	1009
LUSIGNAN,Maud de	246		1241	20	9	138
LUSIGNAN,Raoul de	253			20	18	502
MALTRAVERS,Eleanor	1659	1345	1404	2	7	976
MALTRAVERS,John	1663	1290	1364	2	28	978
MALTRAVERS,Sir John	1660		1348	2	14	977
MALTRAVERS,Sir John	1664			10	2	
MANCHESNE,Joan	1639			3	19	
MARGARET	106			11	13	
MARGARET,of Hainaut	594	1202	1280	16	5	323
MARGARET,Princess	1582	1273	1299	4	23	935
MARGARITE,of Lorraine	598	1140	1194	16	21	818
MARGUERITE,of Foucigny	642	1180	1236	8	23	1008
MARIA	1691	1182	1218	14	13	998
MARIE,Countess	1032	1199	1250	13	7	592
MARIE,of Champagne	596	1174	1204	16	11	984
MARIE,of France	1674	1145	1198	15	17	985
MARIE,Princess	1576	1131	1180	16	31	932
MARIE,Princess	1584	1257	1323	19	3	936
MARSHALL,Eve	256			6	23	97
MARSHALL,Isabella	368		1240	23	9	97
MARSHALL,Maud	178		1248	7	9	97
MARSHALL,William	179	1153	1219	7	18	99
MARY,of Germany	1509	1201	1235	8	15	885
MATILDA	1390			7	21	
MATILDA,de Bar	1738		1275	17	3	1026
MATILDA,de Bourbon	1730	1165	1228	15	21	

The Spear and the Spindle:
Ancestors of Sir Francis Bryan (d. 1550)
Bryan, Bourchier, Bohun, FitzAlan, and Others

Index of Names on Table

Name	RIN	Born/ Chr	Died/ Bur	Chart Number	Person Number	Parent MRIN
MATILDA,de la Roche	1734			16	17	
MATILDA,of Brabant	213	1224	1288	8	7	884
MATILDA/MAUD,"the Empress"	207	1102	1164	12	17	114
MATTHIEU,of Alsace	1577	1137	1173	16	30	
MAUD,of Alsace	1575	1160	1210	8	29	931
MAUD,of Ponthieu	663	1138	1200	13	13	1043
MAUD,of Savoy	1045			13	19	
MAUDIT/MAUDUIT,William	454		1220	9	26	
MAUDUIT,Isabel	232		1268	9	13	253
MECHTILD,of Brabant	1668		1267	16	7	930
MEULLENT,Amice	363		1225	23	17	204
MORTIMER,Isabel de	116			6	5	124
MORTIMER,Joane	234			9	25	388
MORTIMER,Ralph de	705		1246	6	20	388
MORTIMER,Roger de	226	1231	1282	6	10	386
NEWBURGH,Alice de	455			9	27	254
OTTO I,C. of Guelders a	1673		1207	16	26	
PEDRO II,King of Aragon	1692	1176	1213	14	12	347
PETER II,de Courtenay	1028	1155	1219	14	30	689
PETRONILLE,of Chacenay	1746		1161	17	27	
PHILIP II,King of France	631	1165	1223	8	24	344
PHILIP II,King of Germany	1511	1177	1208	8	30	887
PHILIP III,King of France	579	1245	1285	14	2	139
PHILIP IV,King of France	93	1268	1314	4	18	314
PHILIPPA,of Hainault	86	1311	1369	4	5	50
PHILIPPA,of Luxembourg	576			4	21	979
PIERRE/PETER,Prince of France	1200	1125	1183	12	22	423
PLANTAGENET,Anne	1613	1380	1438	1	25	949
PLANTAGENET,Elizabeth Princess	101	1282	1316	4	25	47
PLANTAGENET,Geoffrey V	206	1113	1151	12	16	113
PLANTAGENET,Hameline	191		1202	7	16	1017
PREYERS,Margaret	1635			3	5	974
PREYERS,Sir Thomas	1655			3	10	
QUENCEY,Margaret de	357		1266	23	11	205
QUENCY,Robert de	366		1217	23	22	70
QUENCY,Roger de	58		1264	11	22	70
QUENCY,Saher IV de THE SURETY	128	1154	1219	7	26	78
QUINCEY,Hawise de	134			7	13	70
QUINCEY,Margaret de	611		1280	11	11	42
RAOUL I,de Coucy	1747	1135	1191	17	30	
RENAUD II,C. of Clermont	1775		1162	13	26	
RENAUD II,Count of Bar	1743	1115	1170	17	24	
RIDELISFORD,Emmeline de	216		1276	23	15	119
RIDELISFORD,Walter, Lord de	217		1244	23	30	1016
ROBERT I,Count of Artois	129	1216	1250	8	6	342
ROBERT I,Count of Dreux	1395	1123	1188	17	28	423

The Spear and the Spindle:
Ancestors of Sir Francis Bryan (d. 1550)
Bryan, Bourchier, Bohun, FitzAlan, and Others   Index of Names on Table

Name	RIN	Born/ Chr	Died/ Bur	Chart Number	Person Number	Parent MRIN
ROBERT II, Count of Dreux	1393	1154	1218	17	14	824
ROHESE, of Dover	1714		1264	11	19	1012
SAARBRUCKEN, Sophia von	1752	1150		17	9	1034
SABRAN, Raimon de	1725	1155	1224	12	26	
SAFFENBURG, Matilda von	1754		1145	17	17	1033
SALUZZO, Alasia de	112		1292	6	3	64
SANCHA, of Castile	1569	1140	1177	15	19	597
SANCHA, of Castile	640	1154	1208	12	25	596
SANCHO III, King of Castile	1043	1134	1158	13	20	597
SANCHO VI, King of Navarre	1568	1132	1194	15	18	867
SAUNFORD/SANFORD, Alice	122		1312	7	7	126
SAUNFORD/SANFORD, Gilbert de	229			7	14	
SIMON I, Count of Saarbrucken	1756	1120	1181	17	18	
SPONHEIM, Matilda von	1757	1127		17	19	
STEPHEN V, King of Hungary	1586	1239	1272	19	6	937
TAILLEFER, Aymer de	622	1160	1202	7	22	340
TAILLEFER, William IV de	624		1178	12	20	687
THEOBALD I, Count of Briery	1741	1160	1214	17	12	1028
THEOBALD IV, of Navarre	1564	1201	1253	15	4	926
THIBAULT III, of Navarre	1567	1179	1201	15	8	984
THOMAS I, of Savoy	641	1177	1232	8	22	349
THOMAS, of Woodstock	1611	1354	1397	4	2	45
TOMMASO I, Marquis	117			6	6	
TURENNE, Marguerite de	1199	1120		12	21	703
TYLNEY, Elizabeth	1620		1497	1	7	954
TYLNEY, Sir Frederick	1621			1	14	
URRACA, of Portugal	652	1150	1178	13	9	600
VAUDEMONT, Agnes de	1396	1130	1218	17	29	825
VERDUN, Rohese de	166			6	19	90
VERE, Hugh de	133	1210	1263	7	12	74
VERE, Joan de	114		1293	7	3	66
VERE, Robert de	121	1240	1296	7	6	72
VERE, Robert de THE SURETY	137		1221	7	24	75
WALERAN IV, Duke of Monschou	1749		1226	17	4	1030
WARENNE, Alice de	60		1338	2	25	62
WARREN, Isabel Countess	192		1203	7	17	106
WARREN, John de	119		1304	7	4	98
WARREN, William de	113	1256	1285	7	2	65
WARREN, William de Plantagenet	181		1240	7	8	104
WILLIAM I, Count of Holland a	1671	1174	1222	16	12	981
WILLIAM I, of Geneva	1709			12	30	
WILLIAM II, Talvas	1033	1179	1221	13	14	593
WILLIAM VIII, de Montpellier	1694	1158	1218	14	26	
WILLIAM X, Duke of Acquitaine	212		1137	12	18	405
WITTESBACH, Richardis von	972		1231	16	27	
YOLANDE, of Flanders	1027			14	31	324

The Spear and the Spindle:
Ancestors of Sir Francis Bryan (d. 1550)
Bryan, Bourchier, Bohun, FitzAlan, and Others

Index of Names on Table

Name	RIN	Born/ Chr	Died/ Bur	Chart Number	Person Number	Parent MRIN
YOLANDE, of Hungary	1442	1213	1251	14	7	1018
ZOUCHE, Alan la Ceoche La Coche	259		1190	11	24	142
ZOUCHE, Eudo la	1180		1279	11	6	58
ZOUCHE, Eve la	1177		1314	11	3	679
ZOUCHE, Roger la	107		1238	11	12	141

The Spear and the Spindle:
Ancestors of Sir Francis Bryan (d. 1550)
Bryan, Bourchier, Bohun, FitzAlan, and Others

Index of Names on Table

The Spear and the Spindle:
Ancestors of Sir Francis Bryan (d. 1550)
Bryan, Bourchier, Bohun, FitzAlan, and Others

Genealogical Table

Chart No. 1

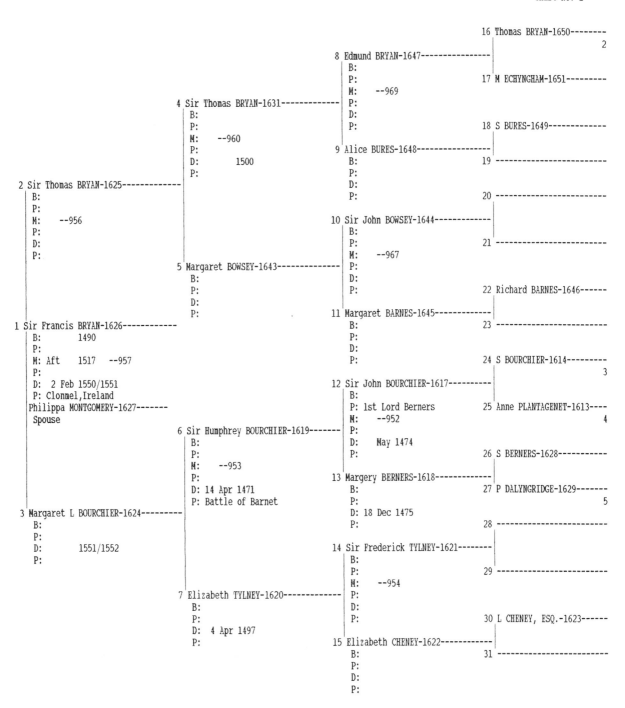

The Spear and the Spindle:
Ancestors of Sir Francis Bryan (d. 1550)
Bryan, Bourchier, Bohun, FitzAlan, and Others

Genealogical Table

Chart No. 2

Number 1 on this chart is the same as no. 16 on chart no. 1

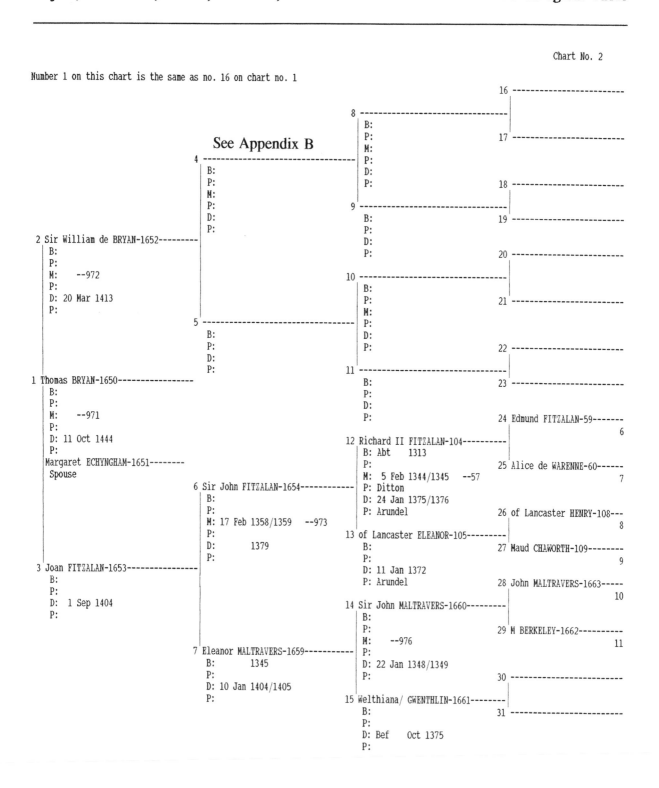

See Appendix B

16 ------------------------

8 ------------------------------
   B:
   P: 17 ------------------------
   M:
4 ------------------------------   P:
   B: D:
   P: P: 18 ------------------------
   M:
   P: 9 ------------------------------
   D: B: 19 ------------------------
   P: P:
2 Sir William de BRYAN-1652---------   D:
   B: P: 20 ------------------------
   P:
   M: --972
   P: 10 -----------------------------
   D: 20 Mar 1413   B:
   P: P: 21 ------------------------
                          M:
5 ------------------------------   P:
   B: D:
   P: P: 22 ------------------------
   D:
   P: 11 -----------------------------
1 Thomas BRYAN-1650----------------   23 ------------------------
   B: B:
   P: P:
   M: --971   D:
   P: P: 24 Edmund FITZALAN-59-------
   D: 11 Oct 1444   12 Richard II FITZALAN-104----------   6
   P: B: Abt   1313
Margaret ECHYNGHAM-1651--------   P: 25 Alice de WARENNE-60-----
   Spouse   M: 5 Feb 1344/1345 --57   7
                          P: Ditton
              6 Sir John FITZALAN-1654------------ D: 24 Jan 1375/1376
                B: P: Arundel   26 of Lancaster HENRY-108---
                P: 8
                M: 17 Feb 1358/1359 --973   13 of Lancaster ELEANOR-105---------
                P: B: 27 Maud CHAWORTH-109--------
                D: 1379   P: 9
                P: D: 11 Jan 1372
3 Joan FITZALAN-1653----------------   P: Arundel   28 John MALTRAVERS-1663-----
   B: 10
   P: 14 Sir John MALTRAVERS-1660--------
   D: 1 Sep 1404   B:
   P: P: 29 M BERKELEY-1662----------
                            M: --976   11
              7 Eleanor MALTRAVERS-1659---------- P:
                B: 1345   D: 22 Jan 1348/1349
                P: P: 30 ------------------------
                D: 10 Jan 1404/1405
                P: 15 Welthiana/ GWENTHLIN-1661-------
                                    B: 31 ------------------------
                                  P:
                                D: Bef   Oct 1375
                                P:

Genealogical Table

The Spear and the Spindle:
Ancestors of Sir Francis Bryan (d. 1550)
Bryan, Bourchier, Bohun, FitzAlan, and Others

Chart No. 3

Number 1 on this chart is the same as no. 24 on chart no. 1

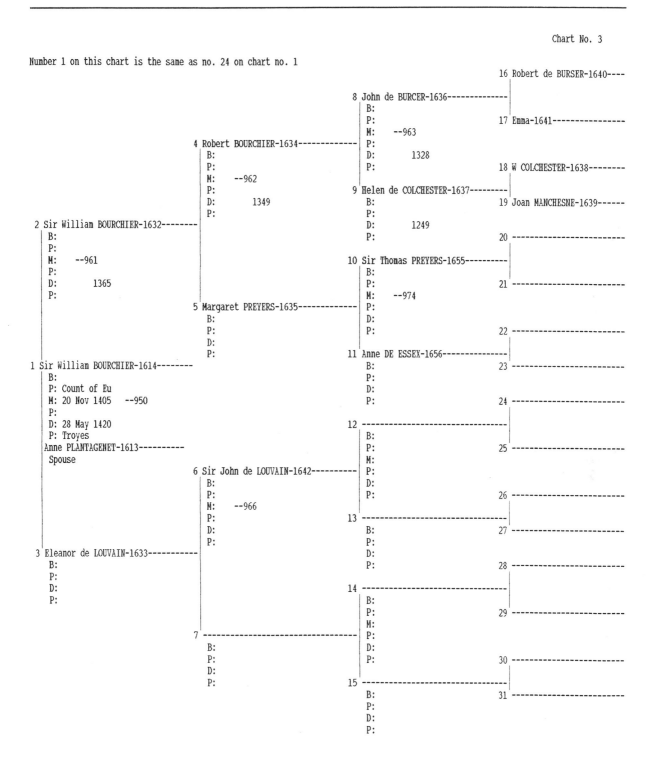

```
                                                                                16 Robert de BURSER-1640----
                                                   8 John de BURCER-1636-------------
                                                     |B:
                                                     |P:                             17 Emma-1641----------------
                                                     |M:     --963
                                4 Robert BOURCHIER-1634-------------|P:
                                  |B:                |D:        1328
                                  |P:                |P:                             18 W COLCHESTER-1638--------
                                  |M:     --962
                                  |P:              9 Helen de COLCHESTER-1637--------
                                  |D:        1349    |B:                             19 Joan MANCHESNE-1639------
                                  |P:                |P:
                                                     |D:        1249
       2 Sir William BOURCHIER-1632--------|         |P:                             20 ------------------------
         |B:
         |P:                                       10 Sir Thomas PREYERS-1655--------
         |M:     --961                               |B:
         |P:                                         |P:                             21 ------------------------
         |D:        1365                             |M:     --974
         |P:                                         |P:
                                5 Margaret PREYERS-1635-------------|D:
                                  |B:                |P:                             22 ------------------------
                                  |P:
                                  |D:              11 Anne DE ESSEX-1656-------------
                                  |P:                |B:                             23 ------------------------
                                                     |P:
                                                     |D:
       1 Sir William BOURCHIER-1614--------|         |P:                             24 ------------------------
         |B:
         |P: Count of Eu                           12 ------------------------------
         |M: 20 Nov 1405    --950                    |B:
         |P:                                         |P:                             25 ------------------------
         |D: 28 May 1420                             |M:
         |P: Troyes                                  |P:
          Anne PLANTAGENET-1613----------          6 Sir John de LOUVAIN-1642----------|D:
          Spouse                                     |B:                              |P:                              26 ------------------------
                                                     |P:
                                                     |M:     --966                  13 ------------------------------
                                                     |P:                             |B:                              27 ------------------------
                                                     |D:                             |P:
                                                     |P:                             |D:
       3 Eleanor de LOUVAIN-1633----------|                                          |P:                              28 ------------------------
         |B:
         |P:                                        14 ------------------------------
         |D:                                         |B:
         |P:                                         |P:                             29 ------------------------
                                                     |M:
                                   7 ------------------------------------|P:
                                     |B:             |D:
                                     |P:             |P:                             30 ------------------------
                                     |D:
                                     |P:           15 ------------------------------
                                                     |B:                             31 ------------------------
                                                     |P:
                                                     |D:
                                                     |P:
```

The Spear and the Spindle:
Ancestors of Sir Francis Bryan (d. 1550)
Bryan, Bourchier, Bohun, FitzAlan, and Others

Genealogical Table

Chart No. 4

Number 1 on this chart is the same as no. 25 on chart no. 1

```
                                                                        16 K EDWARD I-89------------
                                                                                                 12
                                                 8 King of England EDWARD II-87-----
                                                   B: 25 Apr 1284
                                                   P: Carnarvon,Castle,Wales   17 of Castile ELEANOR-90----
                                                   M: 25 Jan 1308    --46                         13
                     4 King of England EDWARD III-85-----  P: Church of Notre,D,,France
                       B: 13 Nov 1312                 D: 21 Sep 1327
                       P: Windsor Castle              P: Berkeley Castle,G        18 K PHILIP IV-93-----------
                       M: 24 Jan 1328    --45                                                     14
                       P: York Minster           9 of France ISABELLA-88------------
                       D: 21 Jun 1377               B:       1292/1295           19 de Navarre JEANNE-578----
                       P: Shene Palace,R,Surrey)     P: Paris(?)                                  15
 2 of Woodstock THOMAS-1611----------                 D: 22 Aug 1358
   B: 7 Jan 1354/1355                                 P: Castle Rising,Norfolk   20 John II D'AVESNES-575----
   P: Woodstock,co. Oxford                                                                        16
   M: Abt    1376    --949                        10 William III D' AVESNES-94--------
   P:                                                B: Abt    1286
   D: Abt    1397                                    P: Hainault,Belgium         21 o PHILIPPA-576-----------
   P: Calais,France                                  M: 19 May 1305    --50                       17
                     5 of Hainault PHILIPPA-86-----------  P:
                       B: 24 Jun 1311               D: 7 Jun 1337
                       P: Valenciennes              P: Valencinnes             22 C CHARLES-1583-----------
                       D: Abt 15 Aug 1369                                                         18
                       P: Windsor Castle,B,England 11 of Valois JEANE-577--------------
 1 Anne PLANTAGENET-1613-------------                 B: Abt    1294           23 Princess MARGARET-1582---
   B:       1380                                      P: Valois,France                            19
   P:                                                 D: 7 Mar 1342/1352
   M: 20 Nov 1405    --950                            P:                        24 H BOHUN VIII-100---------
   P:                                                                                             20
   D: 16 Oct 1438                                 12 William BOHUN-98----------------
   P:                                                B: Abt    1310
   Sir William BOURCHIER-1614-----                   P:                          25 E PLANTAGENET-101--------
   Spouse                                            M:       1338    --53                        21
                     6 Humphrey BOHUN IX-1615------------   P:
                       B:                            D: 16 Sep 1360
                       P:                            P:                          26 B BADLESMERE-103---------
                       M:    --951                                                                22
                       P:                        13 Elizabeth BADLESMERE-99----------
                       D:       1372                 B: Abt    1313             27 Margaret de CLARE-244----
                       P:                            P:                                           23
                                                     D: 8 Jun 1355/1356
 3 Alianore/Eleanor BOHUN-1612-------                 P:                         28 Edmund FITZALAN-59-------
   B:                                                                              Same as no. 24
   P:                                                                              on chart no. 2
   D: 3 Oct 1399                                  14 Richard II FITZALAN-104----------
   P:
                                                  This person is the same person 29 Alice de WARENNE-60------
                                                  as no. 12 on chart no. 2        Same as no. 25
                                                                                  on chart no. 2
                     7 Joan FITZALAN-1616----------------
                       B:                                                        30 of Lancaster HENRY-108---
                       P:                                                          Same as no. 26
                       D:                                                          on chart no. 2
                       P:                        15 of Lancaster ELEANOR-105--------
                                                                                 31 Maud CHAWORTH-109-------
                                                  This person is the same person   Same as no. 27
                                                  as no. 13 on chart no. 2         on chart no. 2
```

Genealogical Table

The Spear and the Spindle:
Ancestors of Sir Francis Bryan (d. 1550)
Bryan, Bourchier, Bohun, FitzAlan, and Others

Chart No. 5

Number 1 on this chart is the same as no. 27 on chart no. 1

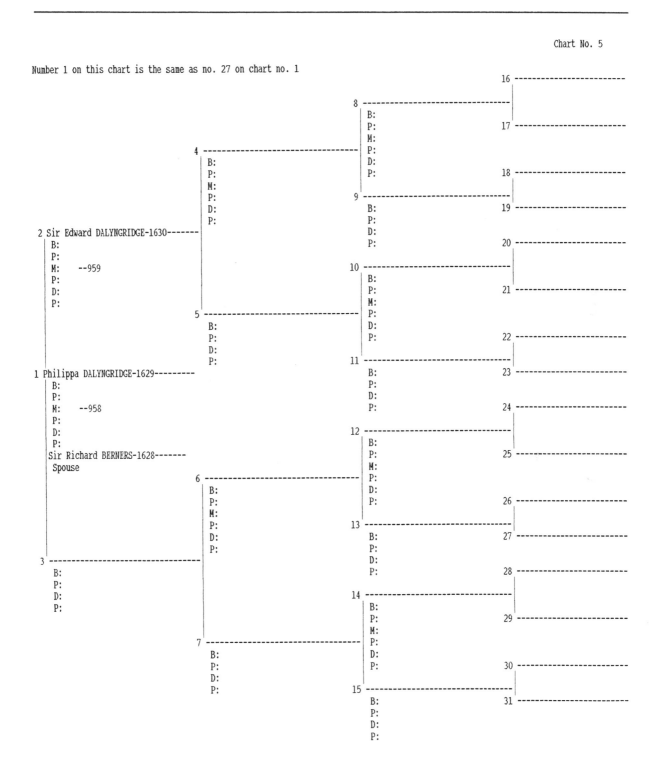

The Spear and the Spindle:
Ancestors of Sir Francis Bryan (d. 1550)
Bryan, Bourchier, Bohun, FitzAlan, and Others

Genealogical Table

Chart No. 6

Number 1 on this chart is the same as no. 24 on chart no. 2

```
                                                                        16 John I FITZALAN-157------

                                              8 John II FITZALAN-155-------------
                                                 B:
                                                 P:                     17 Isabel D'AUBIGNY-158-----
                                                 M:     --84
                          4 John III FITZALAN-115------------  P:
                             B: 14 Sep 1246                    D: Bef 10 Nov 1267
                             P:                                P:                     18 T BOTILLER-165-----------
                             M:     --63
                             P:                            9 Maud le BOTILLER-156------------
                             D: 18 Mar 1271/1272              B:                      19 Rohese de VERDUN-166-----
                             P:                               P:
  2 Richard I FITZALAN-111------------                        D: 27 Nov 1283
     B:  3 Feb 1266/1267                                      P:                      20 Ralph de MORTIMER-705----
     P:
     M: Bef    1285    --55                               10 Roger de MORTIMER-226-----------
     P:                                                      B: Abt    1231
     D:  9 Mar 1301/1302                                     P:                       21 Gladys D DHU-704---------
     P:                                                      M:        1247    --124
                          5 Isabel de MORTIMER-116-----------  P:
                             B:                               D: Bef 10 Oct 1282
                             P:                               P: Kingsland,co. Hereford   22 W BRIOUZE/BRAOS-228------
                             D:
                             P: Living in 1300           11 Maud de BRIOUZE-227-------------
                                                             B:                       23 Eve MARSHALL-256---------
1 Edmund FITZALAN-59----------------                         P:
   B:  1 May 1285                                            D: Bef 23 Mar 1300/1301
   P:                                                        P:                       24 -----------------------
   M:        1305    --31
   P:                                                     12 ------------------------------
   D: 17 Nov 1326                                            B:
   P: Hereford                                               P:                       25 -----------------------
Alice de WARENNE-60-----------                               M:
   Spouse                                                    P:
                          6 Marquis TOMMASO I-117-------------  D:
                             B:                               P:                       26 -----------------------
                             P:
                             M:     --64                  13 ------------------------------
                             P:                              B:                       27 -----------------------
                             D:                              P:
                             P:                              D:
3 Alasia de SALUZZO-112-------------                         P:                       28 -----------------------
   B:
   P:                                                     14 of Ceva/Cave GEORGE-1710---------
   D: 25 Sep 1292                                            B:
   P:                                                        P:                       29 -----------------------
                                                             M:     --1009
                          7 of Ceva/Cave LUISA-118------------  P:
                             B:                               D:
                             P:                               P:                       30 -----------------------
                             D:
                             P:                           15 ------------------------------
                                                             B:                       31 -----------------------
                                                             P:
                                                             D:
                                                             P:
```

16

Genealogical Table

The Spear and the Spindle:
Ancestors of Sir Francis Bryan (d. 1550)
Bryan, Bourchier, Bohun, FitzAlan, and Others

Chart No. 7

Number 1 on this chart is the same as no. 25 on chart no. 2

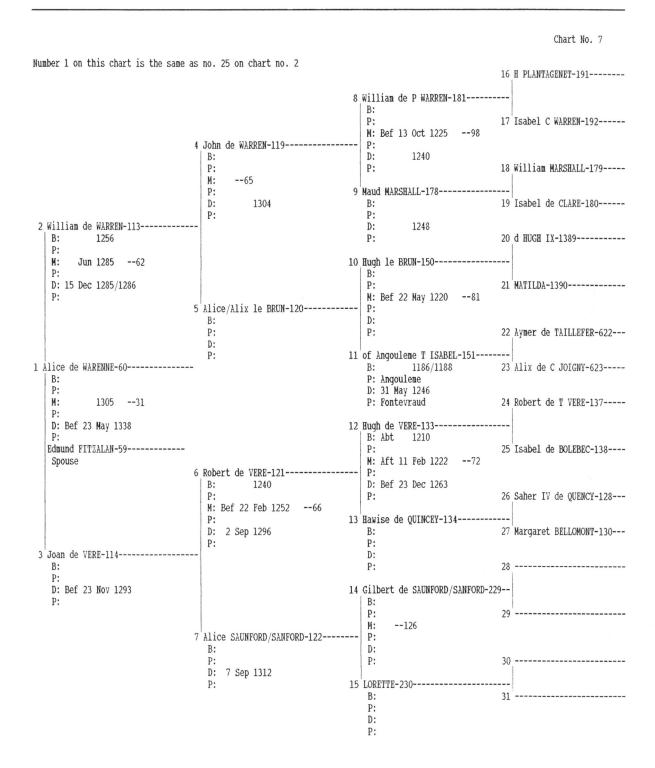

```
                                                                    16 H PLANTAGENET-191--------

                                            8 William de P WARREN-181----------
                                              B:
                                              P:                    17 Isabel C WARREN-192------
                                              M: Bef 13 Oct 1225   --98
                      4 John de WARREN-119--------------- P:
                        B:                    D:      1240
                        P:                    P:                    18 William MARSHALL-179-----
                        M:    --65
                        P:                  9 Maud MARSHALL-178----------------
                        D:      1304          B:                    19 Isabel de CLARE-180------
                        P:                    P:
   2 William de WARREN-113------------        D:      1248
     B:       1256                            P:                    20 d HUGH IX-1389-----------
     P:
     M:     Jun 1285   --62                 10 Hugh le BRUN-150----------------
     P:                                       B:
     D: 15 Dec 1285/1286                      P:                    21 MATILDA-1390------------
     P:                                       M: Bef 22 May 1220   --81
                      5 Alice/Alix le BRUN-120----------- P:
                        B:                    D:
                        P:                    P:                    22 Aymer de TAILLEFER-622---
                        D:
                        P:                  11 of Angouleme T ISABEL-151-------
 1 Alice de WARENNE-60---------------         B:       1186/1188    23 Alix de C JOIGNY-623-----
   B:                                         P: Angouleme
   P:                                         D: 31 May 1246
   M:       1305   --31                       P: Fontevraud         24 Robert de T VERE-137-----
   P:
   D: Bef 23 May 1338                       12 Hugh de VERE-133----------------
   P:                                         B: Abt    1210
   Edmund FITZALAN-59------------              P:                   25 Isabel de BOLEBEC-138----
   Spouse                                     M: Aft 11 Feb 1222   --72
                      6 Robert de VERE-121--------------- P:
                        B:       1240         D: Bef 23 Dec 1263
                        P:                    P:                    26 Saher IV de QUENCY-128---
                        M: Bef 22 Feb 1252   --66
                        P:                  13 Hawise de QUINCEY-134-----------
                        D:  2 Sep 1296        B:                    27 Margaret BELLOMONT-130---
                        P:                    P:
                                              D:
 3 Joan de VERE-114-----------------          P:                    28 -----------------------
   B:
   P:                                       14 Gilbert de SAUNFORD/SANFORD-229--
   D: Bef 23 Nov 1293                         B:
   P:                                         P:                    29 -----------------------
                                              M:    --126
                      7 Alice SAUNFORD/SANFORD-122------- P:
                        B:                    D:
                        P:                    P:                    30 -----------------------
                        D:  7 Sep 1312
                        P:                  15 LORETTE-230--------------------
                                              B:                    31 -----------------------
                                              P:
                                              D:
                                              P:
```

The Spear and the Spindle:
Ancestors of Sir Francis Bryan (d. 1550)
Bryan, Bourchier, Bohun, FitzAlan, and Others

Number 1 on this chart is the same as no. 26 on chart no. 2

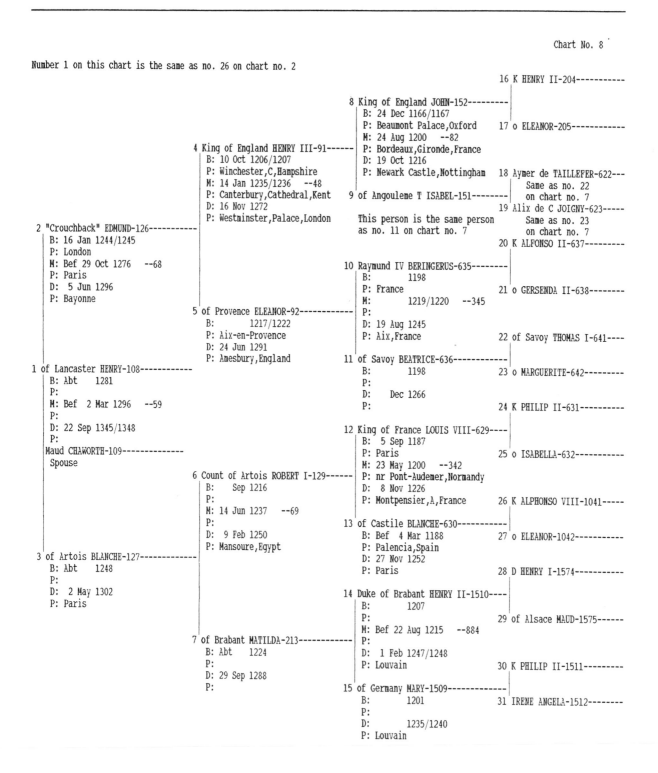

16 K HENRY II-204-----------

8 King of England JOHN-152---------
  B: 24 Dec 1166/1167
  P: Beaumont Palace,Oxford
  M: 24 Aug 1200   --82   17 o ELEANOR-205-----------
  P: Bordeaux,Gironde,France
  D: 19 Oct 1216
  P: Newark Castle,Nottingham   18 Aymer de TAILLEFER-622---
                                    Same as no. 22
4 King of England HENRY III-91------   on chart no. 7
  B: 10 Oct 1206/1207
  P: Winchester,C,Hampshire   19 Alix de C JOIGNY-623-----
  M: 14 Jan 1235/1236   --48   Same as no. 23
  P: Canterbury,Cathedral,Kent   9 of Angouleme T ISABEL-151-------   on chart no. 7
  D: 16 Nov 1272
  P: Westminster,Palace,London   This person is the same person
                                 as no. 11 on chart no. 7
                                                                20 K ALFONSO II-637---------
2 "Crouchback" EDMUND-126-----------
  B: 16 Jan 1244/1245
  P: London
  M: Bef 29 Oct 1276   --68   10 Raymund IV BERINGERUS-635--------
  P: Paris   B: 1198
  D: 5 Jun 1296   P: France   21 o GERSENDA II-638--------
  P: Bayonne   M: 1219/1220   --345
                                    P:
                               5 of Provence ELEANOR-92------------
                                 B: 1217/1222
                                 P: Aix-en-Provence
                                 D: 24 Jun 1291
                                 P: Amesbury,England   D: 19 Aug 1245
                                                       P: Aix,France   22 of Savoy THOMAS I-641----
                                                11 of Savoy BEATRICE-636-----------
                                                   B: 1198
1 of Lancaster HENRY-108------------   P: 23 o MARGUERITE-642---------
  B: Abt   1281   D: Dec 1266
  P: P:
  M: Bef 2 Mar 1296   --59   24 K PHILIP II-631----------
  P:
  D: 22 Sep 1345/1348   12 King of France LOUIS VIII-629----
  P: B: 5 Sep 1187
Maud CHAWORTH-109--------------   P: Paris   25 o ISABELLA-632-----------
  Spouse   M: 23 May 1200   --342
                                                  P: nr Pont-Audemer,Normandy
                               6 Count of Artois ROBERT I-129------ D: 8 Nov 1226
                                 B: Sep 1216   P: Montpensier,A,France   26 K ALPHONSO VIII-1041-----
                                 P:
                                 M: 14 Jun 1237   --69
                                 P: 13 of Castile BLANCHE-630-----------
                                 D: 9 Feb 1250   B: Bef 4 Mar 1188   27 o ELEANOR-1042-----------
                                 P: Mansoure,Egypt   P: Palencia,Spain
                                                                D: 27 Nov 1252
3 of Artois BLANCHE-127------------   P: Paris   28 D HENRY I-1574-----------
  B: Abt   1248
  P:
  D: 2 May 1302   14 Duke of Brabant HENRY II-1510----
  P: Paris   B: 1207
                                                 P: 29 of Alsace MAUD-1575------
                                                 M: Bef 22 Aug 1215   --884
                               7 of Brabant MATILDA-213------------ P:
                                 B: Abt   1224   D: 1 Feb 1247/1248
                                 P: P: Louvain   30 K PHILIP II-1511---------
                                 D: 29 Sep 1288
                                 P: 15 of Germany MARY-1509-------------
                                                                B: 1201   31 IRENE ANGELA-1512--------
                                                                P:
                                                                D: 1235/1240
                                                                P: Louvain

18

Genealogical Table

The Spear and the Spindle:
Ancestors of Sir Francis Bryan (d. 1550)
Bryan, Bourchier, Bohun, FitzAlan, and Others

Chart No. 9

Number 1 on this chart is the same as no. 27 on chart no. 2

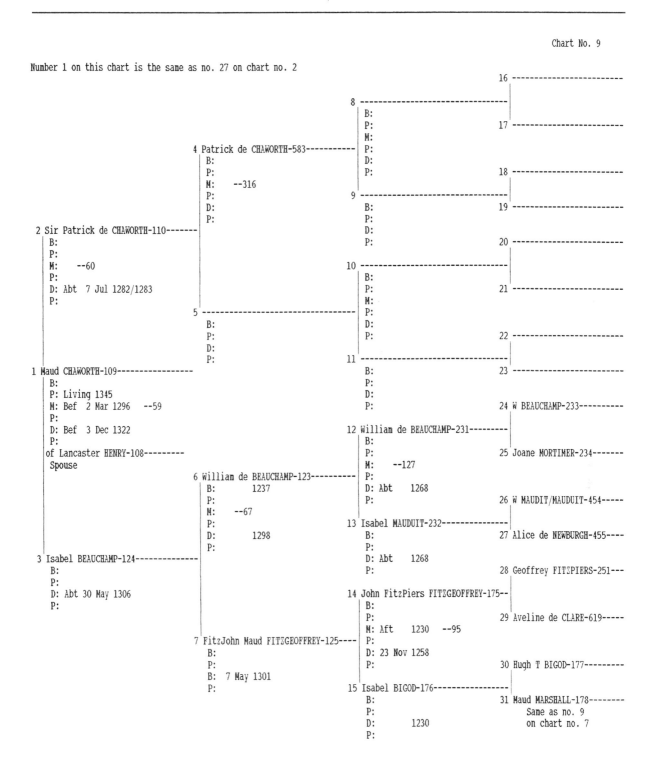

```
                                                                        16 ------------------------
                                                 8 ------------------------------
                                                   B:
                                                   P:                    17 ------------------------
                                                   M:
                  4 Patrick de CHAWORTH-583-----------  P:
                    B:                                 D:
                    P:                                 P:                18 ------------------------
                    M:     --316
                    P:                           9 ------------------------------
                    D:                             B:                    19 ------------------------
                    P:                             P:
                                                   D:
  2 Sir Patrick de CHAWORTH-110------              P:                    20 ------------------------
    B:
    P:
    M:     --60                                 10 ------------------------------
    P:                                            B:
    D: Abt  7 Jul 1282/1283                       P:                     21 ------------------------
    P:                                            M:
                           5 ------------------------------  P:
                             B:                             D:
                             P:                             P:           22 ------------------------
                             D:
                             P:                 11 ------------------------------
  1 Maud CHAWORTH-109-----------------            B:                     23 ------------------------
    B:                                            P:
    P: Living 1345                                D:
    M: Bef  2 Mar 1296    --59                    P:                     24 W BEAUCHAMP-233----------
    P:
    D: Bef  3 Dec 1322                         12 William de BEAUCHAMP-231---------
    P:                                            B:
    of Lancaster HENRY-108---------                P:                    25 Joane MORTIMER-234-------
    Spouse                                         M:     --127
                           6 William de BEAUCHAMP-123----------  P:
                             B:          1237              D: Abt     1268
                             P:                             P:          26 W MAUDIT/MAUDUIT-454-----
                             M:     --67
                             P:                 13 Isabel MAUDUIT-232--------------
                             D:          1298     B:                    27 Alice de NEWBURGH-455----
                             P:                    P:
                                                   D: Abt     1268
  3 Isabel BEAUCHAMP-124--------------             P:                   28 Geoffrey FITZPIERS-251---
    B:
    P:                                         14 John FitzPiers FITZGEOFFREY-175--
    D: Abt 30 May 1306                            B:
    P:                                            P:                    29 Aveline de CLARE-619-----
                                                  M: Aft     1230    --95
                                                  P:
                           7 FitzJohn Maud FITZGEOFFREY-125----  D: 23 Nov 1258
                             B:                             P:          30 Hugh T BIGOD-177---------
                             P:
                             B:   7 May 1301    15 Isabel BIGOD-176----------------
                             P:                    B:                   31 Maud MARSHALL-178-------
                                                   P:                      Same as no. 9
                                                   D:        1230          on chart no. 7
                                                   P:
```

The Spear and the Spindle:
Ancestors of Sir Francis Bryan (d. 1550)
Bryan, Bourchier, Bohun, FitzAlan, and Others

Genealogical Table

Number 1 on this chart is the same as no. 28 on chart no. 2

```
                                                                    16 ----------------------------
                                               8 -------------------------------------
                                                                    B:
                                                                    P:         17 ----------------------------
                                                                    M:
                             4 --------------------------------     P:
                               B:                                   D:
                               P:                                   P:         18 ----------------------------
                               M:
                               P:            9 -------------------------------------
                               D:                                   B:         19 ----------------------------
                               P:                                   P:
2 Sir John MALTRAVERS-1664----------                                D:
    B:                                                              P:         20 ----------------------------
    P:
    M:    --978                             10 -------------------------------------
    P:                                                              B:
    D:                                                              P:         21 ----------------------------
    P:                                                              M:
                             5 --------------------------------     P:
                               B:                                   D:
                               P:                                   P:         22 ----------------------------
                               D:
                               P:           11 -------------------------------------
1 John MALTRAVERS-1663--------------                                B:         23 ----------------------------
    B: Abt    1290                                                  P:
    P:                                                              D:
    M:       1313   --977                                           P:         24 ----------------------------
    P:
    D:       1364                           12 -------------------------------------
    P:                                                              B:
Milicent de E BERKELEY-1662----                                     P:         25 ----------------------------
    Spouse                                                          M:
                             6 --------------------------------     P:
                               B:                                   D:
                               P:                                   P:         26 ----------------------------
                               M:
                               P:           13 -------------------------------------
                               D:                                   B:         27 ----------------------------
                               P:                                   P:
3 Eleanor de GORGES-1665-----------                                 D:
    B:                                                              P:         28 ----------------------------
    P:
    D:                                      14 -------------------------------------
    P:                                                              B:
                                                                    P:         29 ----------------------------
                                                                    M:
                             7 --------------------------------     P:
                               B:                                   D:
                               P:                                   P:         30 ----------------------------
                               D:
                               P:           15 -------------------------------------
                                                                    B:         31 ----------------------------
                                                                    P:
                                                                    D:
                                                                    P:
```

Genealogical Table

The Spear and the Spindle:
Ancestors of Sir Francis Bryan (d. 1550)
Bryan, Bourchier, Bohun, FitzAlan, and Others

Chart No. 11

Number 1 on this chart is the same as no. 29 on chart no. 2

```
                                                                            16 -----------------------
                                               8 Maurice de BERKELEY-1712---------
                                                 B:        1218
                                                 P:                                17 -----------------------
                                                 M: Abt 12 Jul 1247    --1010
                      4 Thomas BERKELEY-1178-------------  P:
                        B:                               D:  4 Apr 1281
                        P:                               P:                        18 Richard FITZROY-1713-----
                        M:        1267   --678
                        P:                               9 Isabel FITZROY-1711-------------  19 of Dover ROHESE-1714-----
                        D: 23 Jul 1321                     B:
                        P:                                 P:
  2 Maurice BERKELEY-1176------------                      D:  7 Jul 1276
    B:     Apr 1271/1281                                   P:                        20 W FERRIERES-471----------
    P:
    M:        1289   --677                               10 William de FERRERS-469----------
    P:                                                      B: Abt     1193
    D: 31 May 1326                                          P: 7th Earl of,Derby     21 Agnes o KEVELIOC-472-----
    P:                                                      M:        1238   --332
                      5 Joan FERRERS-1179----------------   P:
                        B:                                  D:        1254
                        P:                                  P: Evington,near Leicester  22 Roger de QUENCY-58-------
                        D: 19 Mar 1309/1310               11 Margaret de QUINCEY-611----------
                        P:                                  B:                        23 of Galloway HELEN-80-----
  1 Milicent de (Ela) BERKELEY-1662---                      P:
    B:                                                      D: Bef 12 Mar 1280/1281
    P:                                                      P:                        24 Alan la C ZOUCHE-259-----
    M:        1313   --977
    P:                                                    12 Roger la ZOUCHE-107-------------
    D: Aft    1322                                          B:
    P:                                                      P:                        25 -----------------------
  John MALTRAVERS-1663-----------                           M:    --58
    Spouse                                                  P:
                      6 Eudo la ZOUCHE-1180---------------   D:        1238
                        B:                                  P:                        26 -----------------------
                        P: liv in 1273
                        M:    --679                       13 MARGARET-106--------------------
                        P:                                  B:                        27 -----------------------
                        D:        1279                      P:
                        P:                                  D:
  3 Eve la ZOUCHE-1177----------------                      P:                        28 W CANTILUPE-1716---------
    B:
    P:                                                    14 William de CANTILUPE-1186-------
    D:        1314                                          B:
    P:                                                      P:                        29 -----------------------
                                                           M: Bef 15 Feb 1247   --682
                      7 Milicent de CANTILUPE-1181-------   P:
                        B:                                  D: 25 Sep 1254
                        P:                                  P:                        30 W BRIOUZE/BRAOS-228------
                        D:                                                               Same as no. 22
                        P:                                15 Eva BRAOS-1187------------------- on chart no. 6
                                                           B:                        31 Eve MARSHALL-256---------
                                                           P:                             Same as no. 23
                                                           D:        1255               on chart no. 6
                                                           P:
```

The Spear and the Spindle:
Ancestors of Sir Francis Bryan (d. 1550)
Bryan, Bourchier, Bohun, FitzAlan, and Others

Genealogical Table

Chart No. 12

Number 1 on this chart is the same as no. 16 on chart no. 4

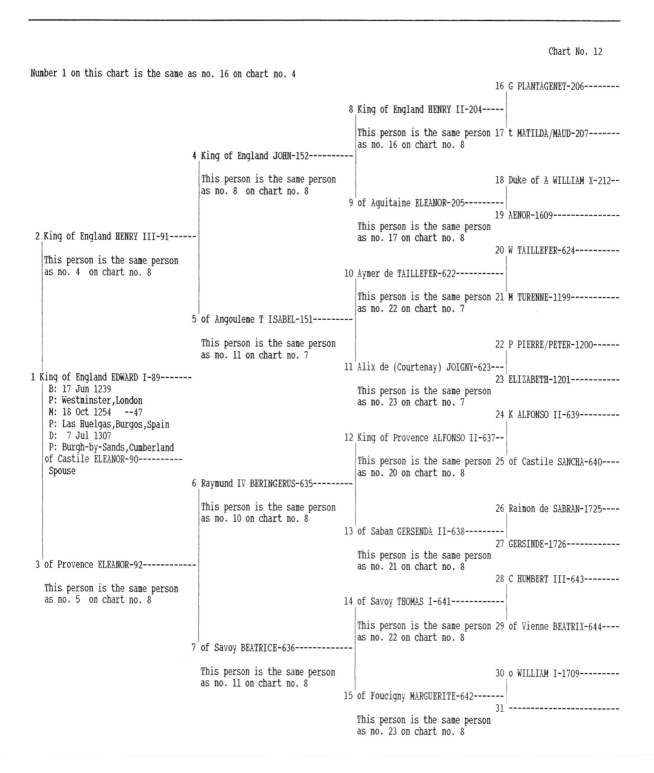

```
                                                                    16 G PLANTAGENET-206--------

                                        8 King of England HENRY II-204-----

                                        This person is the same person  17 t MATILDA/MAUD-207-------
                                        as no. 16 on chart no. 8
               4 King of England JOHN-152----------

               This person is the same person                      18 Duke of A WILLIAM X-212--
               as no. 8 on chart no. 8
                                        9 of Aquitaine ELEANOR-205--------
                                                                    19 AENOR-1609---------------
                                        This person is the same person
                                        as no. 17 on chart no. 8
 2 King of England HENRY III-91------                              20 W TAILLEFER-624----------

 This person is the same person         10 Aymer de TAILLEFER-622-----------
 as no. 4  on chart no. 8
                                        This person is the same person 21 M TURENNE-1199-----------
                                        as no. 22 on chart no. 7
               5 of Angouleme T ISABEL-151---------

               This person is the same person                      22 P PIERRE/PETER-1200------
               as no. 11 on chart no. 7
                                        11 Alix de (Courtenay) JOIGNY-623---
                                                                    23 ELIZABETH-1201-----------
                                        This person is the same person
                                        as no. 23 on chart no. 7
 1 King of England EDWARD I-89-------                               24 K ALFONSO II-639---------
    B: 17 Jun 1239
    P: Westminster,London               12 King of Provence ALFONSO II-637--
    M: 18 Oct 1254   --47
    P: Las Huelgas,Burgos,Spain         This person is the same person 25 of Castile SANCHA-640----
    D:  7 Jul 1307                      as no. 20 on chart no. 8
    P: Burgh-by-Sands,Cumberland
 of Castile ELEANOR-90----------                                   26 Raimon de SABRAN-1725----
    Spouse
               6 Raymund IV BERINGERUS-635---------

               This person is the same person                      27 GERSINDE-1726------------
               as no. 10 on chart no. 8
                                        13 of Saban GERSENDA II-638---------

                                        This person is the same person 28 C HUMBERT III-643--------
                                        as no. 21 on chart no. 8
 3 of Provence ELEANOR-92------------

 This person is the same person         14 of Savoy THOMAS I-641------------
 as no. 5  on chart no. 8
                                        This person is the same person 29 of Vienne BEATRIX-644----
                                        as no. 22 on chart no. 8
               7 of Savoy BEATRICE-636-------------
                                                                    30 o WILLIAM I-1709---------
               This person is the same person
               as no. 11 on chart no. 8
                                        15 of Foucigny MARGUERITE-642-------
                                                                    31 -----------------------
                                        This person is the same person
                                        as no. 23 on chart no. 8
```

22

Genealogical Table

The Spear and the Spindle:
Ancestors of Sir Francis Bryan (d. 1550)
Bryan, Bourchier, Bohun, FitzAlan, and Others

Chart No. 13

Number 1 on this chart is the same as no. 17 on chart no. 4

```
                                                                              16 K ALPHONSO VII-1038------

                                                  8 King of Leon FERNANDO II-651-----
                                                    B:        1137
                                                    P:                                17 o BERENGARIA-1040--------
                                                    M:        1160/1165    --353
                           4 King of Leon ALFONSO IX-649-------  P:
                             B:        1166/1171           D: 22 Jan 1188
                             P: Zamora,Leon,Spain          P: Benavente,Italy         18 K ALPHONSO I-1044--------
                             M: Bef    1190   --352
                             P:                           9 of Portugal URRACA-652----------
                             D: 24 Sep 1229/1230            B: Abt    1150             19 of Savoy MAUD-1045-------
                             P: Villanueva de,Sarria        P:
                                                            D:        1178/1188
2 FERDINAND III-95-----------------                         P: Bamba,Spain            20 K SANCHO III-1043--------
  B:        1191/1201
  P: King of Castile,and Leon                            10 K ALPHONSO VIII-1041------------
  M:        1227/1237    --51
  P: Burgos,Spain                                         This person is the same person 21 of Navarre BLANCHE-735---
  D: 30 May 1252                                          as no. 26 on chart no. 8
  P: Seville
                           5 of Castile BERENGARIA-650---------
                             B:                                                       22 K HENRY II-204-----------
                             P:                                                          Same as no. 16
                             D:        1244                                              on chart no. 8
                             P:                          11 of England ELEANOR-1042----------
1 of Castile ELEANOR-90-------------                                                  23 o ELEANOR-205-----------
  B: Abt    1244                                          This person is the same person   Same as no. 17
  P: Castile,Spain                                        as no. 27 on chart no. 8         on chart no. 8
  M: 18 Oct 1254    --47                                                              24 ALBERIC I-664------------
  P: Las Huelgas,Burgos,Spain
  D: 28 Nov 1290                                         12 ALBERIC II-662------------------
  P: Harby,Nottinghamshire                                B: Abt    1135
King of England EDWARD I-89----                           P:                          25 ------------------------
  Spouse                                                  M:        --360
                           6 Simon de C DAMMARTIN-1031---------  P:
                             B: Abt    1180                D: 19 Sep 1200
                             P:                            P: London                  26 C RENAUD II-1775---------
                             M:        1208/1211    --591
                             P:                          13 of Ponthieu MAUD-663------------
                             D: 21 Sep 1239                B: Abt    1138             27 o CLEMENCE-1774----------
                             P: Abbeville,France           P:
                                                           D: Aft    Oct 1200
3 Joanna DAMMARTIN-96--------------                        P:                          28 Count of P JEAN I-1035---
  B:        1208/1220
  P:                                                     14 Talvas WILLIAM II-1033-----------
  D: 16 Mar 1278/1279                                      B:        1179
  P: Abbeville,France                                      P:                          29 o BEATRICE-1036---------
                                                           M: 20 Aug 1195    --592
                           7 Countess MARIE-1032--------------- P:
                             B: 17 Apr 1199                D: 6 Oct 1221
                             P:                            P:                          30 K LOUIS VII-633----------
                             D:     Sep 1250/1251
                             P:                          15 of France ALICE-1034------------
                                                           B: Abt    1170             31 o ALIX/ADELA/ALICE-634---
                                                           P: France
                                                           D: Aft 18 Jul 1218
                                                           P:
```

The Spear and the Spindle:
Ancestors of Sir Francis Bryan (d. 1550)
Bryan, Bourchier, Bohun, FitzAlan, and Others

Number 1 on this chart is the same as no. 18 on chart no. 4

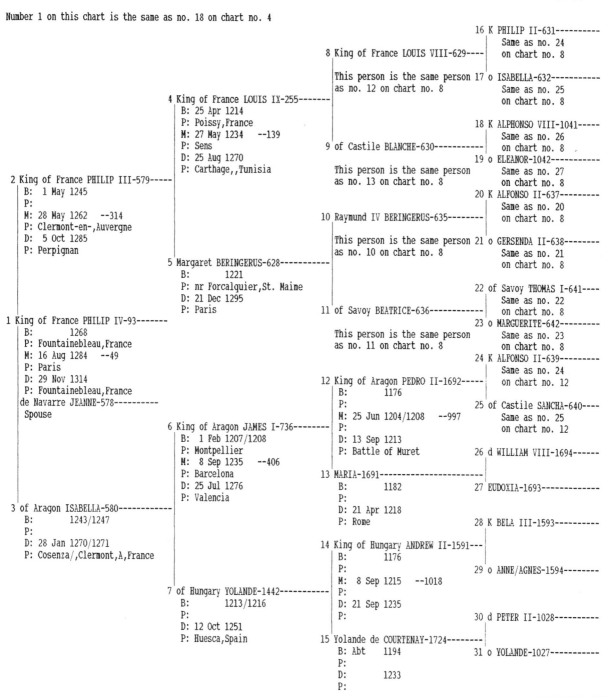

```
                                                                          16 K PHILIP II-631----------
                                                                             Same as no. 24
                                          8 King of France LOUIS VIII-629----  on chart no. 8

                                          This person is the same person  17 o ISABELLA-632-----------
                                          as no. 12 on chart no. 8           Same as no. 25
                   4 King of France LOUIS IX-255-------                      on chart no. 8
                     B: 25 Apr 1214
                     P: Poissy,France                                     18 K ALPHONSO VIII-1041-----
                     M: 27 May 1234   --139                                   Same as no. 26
                     P: Sens                9 of Castile BLANCHE-630----------  on chart no. 8
                     D: 25 Aug 1270
                     P: Carthage,,Tunisia   This person is the same person  19 o ELEANOR-1042-----------
                                            as no. 13 on chart no. 8          Same as no. 27
 2 King of France PHILIP III-579-----                                         on chart no. 8
   B:  1 May 1245                                                          20 K ALFONSO II-637---------
   P:                                                                         Same as no. 20
   M: 28 May 1262   --314                 10 Raymund IV BERINGERUS-635--------  on chart no. 8
   P: Clermont-en-,Auvergne
   D:  5 Oct 1285                          This person is the same person  21 o GERSENDA II-638--------
   P: Perpignan                            as no. 10 on chart no. 8           Same as no. 21
                   5 Margaret BERINGERUS-628-----------                       on chart no. 8
                     B:       1221
                     P: nr Forcalquier,St. Maime                           22 of Savoy THOMAS I-641----
                     D: 21 Dec 1295                                           Same as no. 22
                     P: Paris               11 of Savoy BEATRICE-636-----------  on chart no. 8
 1 King of France PHILIP IV-93-------
   B:       1268                            This person is the same person  23 o MARGUERITE-642---------
   P: Fountainebleau,France                 as no. 11 on chart no. 8          Same as no. 23
   M: 16 Aug 1284   --49                                                      on chart no. 8
   P: Paris                                                                24 K ALFONSO II-639---------
   D: 29 Nov 1314                          12 King of Aragon PEDRO II-1692-----  Same as no. 24
   P: Fountainebleau,France                  B:       1176                    on chart no. 12
 de Navarre JEANNE-578----------             P:
   Spouse                                    M: 25 Jun 1204/1208   --997   25 of Castile SANCHA-640----
                   6 King of Aragon JAMES I-736--------  P:                   Same as no. 25
                     B: 1 Feb 1207/1208     D: 13 Sep 1213                    on chart no. 12
                     P: Montpellier         P: Battle of Muret
                     M:  8 Sep 1235   --406                                26 d WILLIAM VIII-1694------
                     P: Barcelona          13 MARIA-1691--------------------
                     D: 25 Jul 1276           B:       1182                 27 EUDOXIA-1693-------------
                     P: Valencia              P:
 3 of Aragon ISABELLA-580-----------          D: 21 Apr 1218               28 K BELA III-1593----------
   B:       1243/1247                         P: Rome
   P:
   D: 28 Jan 1270/1271                     14 King of Hungary ANDREW II-1591---
   P: Cosenza/,Clermont,A,France              B:       1176
                                              P:                           29 o ANNE/AGNES-1594--------
                                              M:  8 Sep 1215   --1018
                   7 of Hungary YOLANDE-1442-----------  P:
                     B:       1213/1216       D: 21 Sep 1235               30 d PETER II-1028----------
                     P:                       P:
                     D: 12 Oct 1251        15 Yolande de COURTENAY-1724-------
                     P: Huesca,Spain          B: Abt    1194               31 o YOLANDE-1027-----------
                                              P:
                                              D:       1233
                                              P:
```

The Spear and the Spindle:
Ancestors of Sir Francis Bryan (d. 1550)
Bryan, Bourchier, Bohun, FitzAlan, and Others

Genealogical Table

Number 1 on this chart is the same as no. 19 on chart no. 4

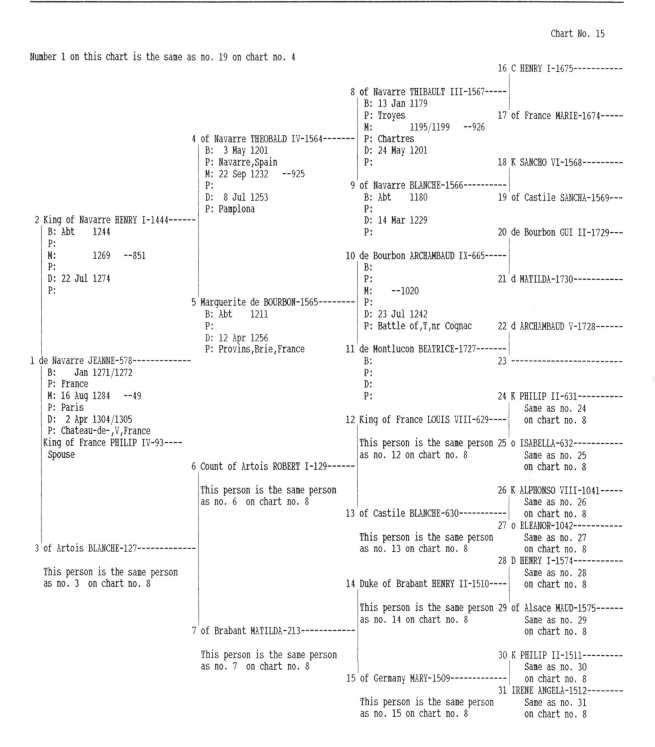

```
                                                                              16 C HENRY I-1675-----------

                                          8 of Navarre THIBAULT III-1567-----
                                            B: 13 Jan 1179
                                            P: Troyes                         17 of France MARIE-1674-----
                                            M:      1195/1199   --926
                 4 of Navarre THEOBALD IV-1564------| P: Chartres
                   B:  3 May 1201                     D: 24 May 1201
                   P: Navarre,Spain                   P:                      18 K SANCHO VI-1568---------
                   M: 22 Sep 1232   --925
                   P:                               9 of Navarre BLANCHE-1566---------
                   D:  8 Jul 1253                     B: Abt     1180         19 of Castile SANCHA-1569---
                   P: Pamplona                        P:
                                                      D: 14 Mar 1229
 2 King of Navarre HENRY I-1444------                 P:                      20 de Bourbon GUI II-1729---
   B: Abt     1244
   P:
   M:       1269   --851                           10 de Bourbon ARCHAMBAUD IX-665-----
   P:                                                 B:                      21 d MATILDA-1730-----------
   D: 22 Jul 1274                                     P:
   P:                                                 M:     --1020
                 5 Marguerite de BOURBON-1565-------- D: 23 Jul 1242
                   B: Abt     1211                    P: Battle of,T,nr Cognac 22 d ARCHAMBAUD V-1728------
                   P:                              11 de Montlucon BEATRICE-1727------
                   D: 12 Apr 1256                     B:                      23 -----------------------
                   P: Provins,Brie,France             P:
 1 de Navarre JEANNE-578------------                  D:
   B:     Jan 1271/1272                               P:                      24 K PHILIP II-631----------
   P: France                                                                     Same as no. 24
   M: 16 Aug 1284   --49                           12 King of France LOUIS VIII-629----  on chart no. 8
   P: Paris
   D:  2 Apr 1304/1305                              This person is the same person 25 o ISABELLA-632----------
   P: Chateau-de-,V,France                          as no. 12 on chart no. 8       Same as no. 25
King of France PHILIP IV-93----                                                    on chart no. 8
   Spouse
                 6 Count of Artois ROBERT I-129------                          26 K ALPHONSO VIII-1041-----
                                                                                  Same as no. 26
                   This person is the same person                              13 of Castile BLANCHE-630----------  on chart no. 8
                   as no. 6  on chart no. 8                                        27 o ELEANOR-1042----------
                                                   This person is the same person  Same as no. 27
 3 of Artois BLANCHE-127------------                as no. 13 on chart no. 8       on chart no. 8
                                                                               28 D HENRY I-1574-----------
   This person is the same person                                                 Same as no. 28
   as no. 3  on chart no. 8                        14 Duke of Brabant HENRY II-1510----  on chart no. 8

                                                   This person is the same person 29 of Alsace MAUD-1575------
                                                    as no. 14 on chart no. 8       Same as no. 29
                 7 of Brabant MATILDA-213------------                              on chart no. 8

                   This person is the same person                              30 K PHILIP II-1511---------
                   as no. 7  on chart no. 8                                       Same as no. 30
                                                   15 of Germany MARY-1509------------  on chart no. 8
                                                                               31 IRENE ANGELA-1512--------
                                                   This person is the same person  Same as no. 31
                                                    as no. 15 on chart no. 8       on chart no. 8
```

The Spear and the Spindle:
Ancestors of Sir Francis Bryan (d. 1550)
Bryan, Bourchier, Bohun, FitzAlan, and Others

Genealogical Table

Chart No. 16

Number 1 on this chart is the same as no. 20 on chart no. 4

```
                                                                    16 N D'AVESNES-1733---------

                                        8 Jacques D'AVESNES-1731-----------
                                          B: Abt     1150
                                          P:                                17 d MATILDA-1734-----------
                                          M:     --1023
                   4 Bouchard D'AVESNES-593------------ P:
                     B: Abt     1180                   D:  7 Sep 1191
                     P:                                P: Battle of Arsouf,P    18 Bernard de GUISE-1735----
                     M: Bef 23 Jul 1212   --322
                     P:                        9 Adele de GUISE-1732-------------
                     D:      1221/1224           B: Abt     1155              19 ADELAIDE/ALIX-1736-------
                     P: Etraeungt,Nord,France    P:
                                                 D:
  2 John I D'AVESNES-581-------------            P:                          20 o BALDWIN V-597----------
    B:  1 May 1218
    P: Etraeungt,Nord,France            10 of Hainaut BALDWIN VI-595-------
    M:  9 Oct 1246   --315                 B:    Jul 1171
    P:                                     P: Valenciennes,France            21 o MARGARITE-598----------
    D: 24 Dec 1255/1257                    M:  6 Jan 1185/1186   --323
    P:                 5 of Hainaut MARGARET-594----------- P:
                         B:  2 Jun 1202                D: 11 Jun 1205/1206
                         P: Constantinople,Turkey     P:                     22 C HENRY I-1675-----------
                         D: 10 Feb 1280                                         Same as no. 16
                         P:                    11 of Champagne MARIE-596-----------  on chart no. 15
  1 John II D'AVESNES-575------------              B:      1174              23 of France MARIE-1674-----
    B:       1247                                  P:                           Same as no. 17
    P: Brabant,Holland                            D:  9 Aug 1204                on chart no. 15
    M:       1270   --313                          P:                        24 C FLORENT III-1670-------
    P:
    D: 22 Aug 1304                         12 Count of Holland WILLIAM I-1671--
    P:                                        B: Abt     1174
  of Luxembourg PHILIPPA-576-----            P:                             25 Ada de HUNTINGDON-1669---
    Spouse                                    M:       1198     --982
                   6 C FLORENT IV-1667---------------- P:
                     B: 24 Jun 1210                   D:      1222/1224
                     P:                               P:                    26 C OTTO I-1673------------
                     M: Bef    Dec 1224   --980
                     P:                        13 of Guelders ADELAIDE-1672-------
                     D:      1234/1245           B: Abt     1186           27 R WITTESBACH-972---------
                     P:                          P:
  3 of Holland ADELAIDE-582-----------           D:  4 Feb 1218
    B: Abt     1225                              P:                         28 C GODFREY III-1704-------
    P:
    D: Abt     1284                        14 Duke of Brabant HENRY I-1574-----
    P:
                                          This person is the same person  29 M LIMBURG-1737-----------
                                          as no. 28 on chart no. 8

                   7 of Brabant MECHTILD-1668----------
                     B:                                                    30 o MATTHIEU-1577----------
                     P:
                     D: 21 Dec 1267
                     P:                        15 of Alsace MAUD-1575-------------
                                                                          31 Princess MARIE-1576------
                                          This person is the same person
                                          as no. 29 on chart no. 8
```

Genealogical Table

The Spear and the Spindle:
Ancestors of Sir Francis Bryan (d. 1550)
Bryan, Bourchier, Bohun, FitzAlan, and Others

Chart No. 17

Number 1 on this chart is the same as no. 21 on chart no. 4

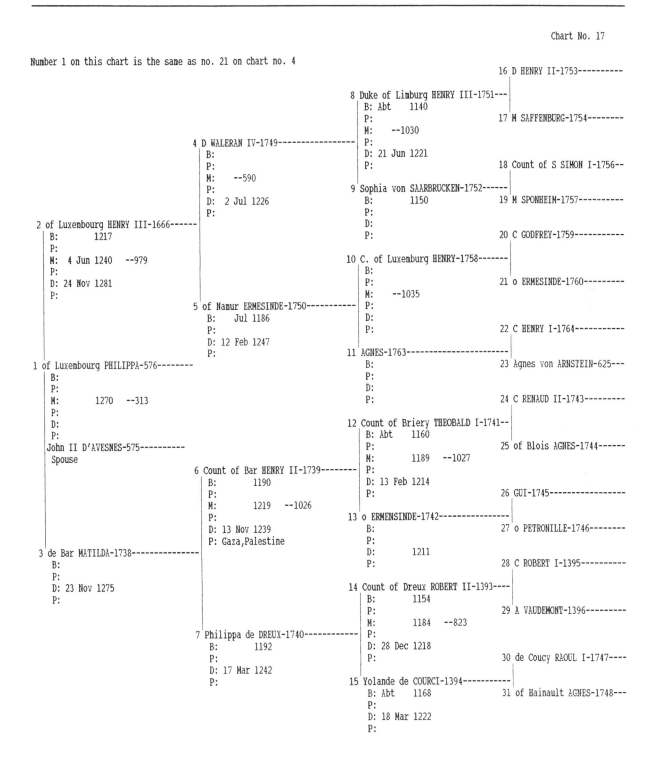

```
                                                                    16 D HENRY II-1753----------

                                             8 Duke of Limburg HENRY III-1751---
                                               B: Abt     1140
                                               P:                               17 M SAFFENBURG-1754--------
                                               M:    --1030
                          4 D WALERAN IV-1749----------------  P:
                            B:                                 D: 21 Jun 1221
                            P:                                 P:                18 Count of S SIMON I-1756--
                            M:    --590
                            P:                               9 Sophia von SAARBRUCKEN-1752-----
                            D: 2 Jul 1226                      B:       1150     19 M SPONHEIM-1757----------
                            P:                                 P:
                                                              D:
  2 of Luxembourg HENRY III-1666------                        P:                20 C GODFREY-1759-----------
    B:       1217
    P:                                                      10 C. of Luxemburg HENRY-1758-------
    M: 4 Jun 1240    --979                                    B:
    P:                                                        P:                21 o ERMESINDE-1760---------
    D: 24 Nov 1281                                            M:    --1035
    P:                          5 of Namur ERMESINDE-1750----------- P:
                                 B:    Jul 1186               D:
                                 P:                           P:                22 C HENRY I-1764-----------
                                 D: 12 Feb 1247
                                 P:                         11 AGNES-1763----------------------
  1 of Luxembourg PHILIPPA-576--------                        B:                23 Agnes von ARNSTEIN-625---
    B:                                                        P:
    P:                                                        D:
    M:       1270    --313                                    P:                24 C RENAUD II-1743---------
    P:
    D:                                                     12 Count of Briery THEOBALD I-1741--
    P:                                                        B: Abt     1160
  John II D'AVESNES-575----------                             P:                25 of Blois AGNES-1744------
    Spouse                                                    M:       1189    --1027
                                6 Count of Bar HENRY II-1739------- P:
                                  B:       1190               D: 13 Feb 1214
                                  P:                          P:                26 GUI-1745-----------------
                                  M:       1219    --1026
                                  P:                        13 o ERMENSINDE-1742---------------
                                  D: 13 Nov 1239              B:                27 o PETRONILLE-1746--------
                                  P: Gaza,Palestine           P:
                                                             D:       1211
  3 de Bar MATILDA-1738--------------                         P:                28 C ROBERT I-1395----------
    B:
    P:                                                      14 Count of Dreux ROBERT II-1393----
    D: 23 Nov 1275                                            B:       1154
    P:                                                        P:                29 A VAUDEMONT-1396---------
                                                             M:       1184    --823
                                                             P:
                                7 Philippa de DREUX-1740------------ D: 28 Dec 1218
                                  B:       1192              P:                 30 de Coucy RAOUL I-1747----
                                  P:
                                  D: 17 Mar 1242           15 Yolande de COURCI-1394----------
                                  P:                          B: Abt     1168   31 of Hainault AGNES-1748---
                                                             P:
                                                             D: 18 Mar 1222
                                                             P:
```

The Spear and the Spindle:
Ancestors of Sir Francis Bryan (d. 1550)
Bryan, Bourchier, Bohun, FitzAlan, and Others

Number 1 on this chart is the same as no. 22 on chart no. 4

```
                                                                    16 K PHILIP II-631----------
                                                                       Same as no. 24
                                          8 King of France LOUIS VIII-629----| on chart no. 8

                                          This person is the same person 17 o ISABELLA-632-----------
                                          as no. 12 on chart no. 8       Same as no. 25
                       4 King of France LOUIS IX-255-------|            on chart no. 8

                       This person is the same person                   18 K ALPHONSO VIII-1041-----
                       as no. 4  on chart no. 14                           Same as no. 26
                                          9 of Castile BLANCHE-630----------|  on chart no. 8
                                                                        19 o ELEANOR-1042-----------
                                          This person is the same person   Same as no. 27
                                          as no. 13 on chart no. 8       on chart no. 8
                                                                        20 K ALFONSO II-637---------
 2 King of France PHILIP III-579-----                                      Same as no. 20
                                         10 Raymund IV BERINGERUS-635--------|  on chart no. 8
 This person is the same person
 as no. 2  on chart no. 14               This person is the same person 21 o GERSENDA II-638--------
                                         as no. 10 on chart no. 8        Same as no. 21
                       5 Margaret BERINGERUS-628-----------              on chart no. 8

                       This person is the same person                   22 of Savoy THOMAS I-641----
                       as no. 5  on chart no. 14                           Same as no. 22
                                         11 of Savoy BEATRICE-636-----------|  on chart no. 8
 1 Count of Valois CHARLES-1583------                                   23 o MARGUERITE-642---------
   B: 12 Mar 1270/1271                    This person is the same person   Same as no. 23
   P: Vincennes,France                    as no. 11 on chart no. 8       on chart no. 8
   M: 16 Aug 1290   --934                                               24 K ALFONSO II-639---------
   P: Corbeil                                                             Same as no. 24
   D: 16 Dec 1325                         12 King of Aragon PEDRO II-1692-----|  on chart no. 12
   P: Paris,France
 Princess MARGARET-1582---------          This person is the same person 25 of Castile SANCHA-640----
   Spouse                                 as no. 12 on chart no. 14       Same as no. 25
                       6 King of Aragon JAMES I-736-------|              on chart no. 12

                       This person is the same person                   26 d WILLIAM VIII-1694------
                       as no. 6  on chart no. 14                           Same as no. 26
                                         13 MARIA-1691----------------------|  on chart no. 14
                                                                        27 EUDOXIA-1693-------------
                                          This person is the same person   Same as no. 27
                                          as no. 13 on chart no. 14      on chart no. 14
                                                                        28 K BELA III-1593----------
 3 of Aragon ISABELLA-580-----------                                      Same as no. 28
                                         14 King of Hungary ANDREW II-1591---|  on chart no. 14
 This person is the same person
 as no. 3  on chart no. 14               This person is the same person 29 o ANNE/AGNES-1594--------
                                         as no. 14 on chart no. 14       Same as no. 29
                       7 of Hungary YOLANDE-1442-----------              on chart no. 14

                       This person is the same person                   30 d PETER II-1028----------
                       as no. 7  on chart no. 14                           Same as no. 30
                                         15 Yolande de COURTENAY-1724--------|  on chart no. 14
                                                                        31 o YOLANDE-1027-----------
                                          This person is the same person   Same as no. 31
                                          as no. 15 on chart no. 14      on chart no. 14
```

28

Genealogical Table

The Spear and the Spindle:
Ancestors of Sir Francis Bryan (d. 1550)
Bryan, Bourchier, Bohun, FitzAlan, and Others

Chart No. 19

Number 1 on this chart is the same as no. 23 on chart no. 4

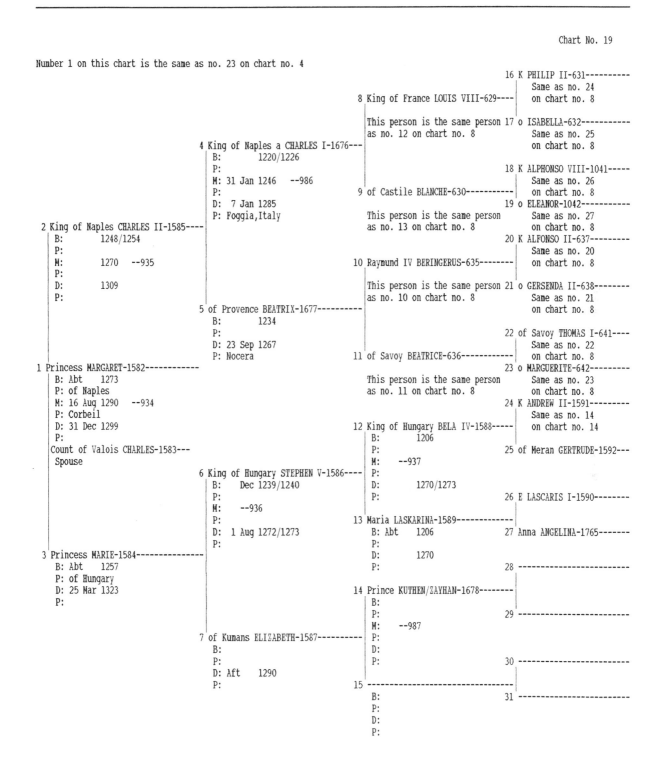

```
                                                                    16 K PHILIP II-631----------
                                                                       Same as no. 24
                                          8 King of France LOUIS VIII-629----  on chart no. 8

                                          This person is the same person 17 o ISABELLA-632-----------
                                          as no. 12 on chart no. 8       Same as no. 25
                                                                         on chart no. 8
                 4 King of Naples a CHARLES I-1676---
                   B:       1220/1226                              18 K ALPHONSO VIII-1041-----
                   P:                                                 Same as no. 26
                   M: 31 Jan 1246   --986                          9 of Castile BLANCHE-630----------  on chart no. 8
                   P:                                                              19 o ELEANOR-1042-----------
                   D:  7 Jan 1285                   This person is the same person    Same as no. 27
                   P: Foggia,Italy                  as no. 13 on chart no. 8          on chart no. 8
 2 King of Naples CHARLES II-1585----                                             20 K ALFONSO II-637---------
    B:      1248/1254                                                                Same as no. 20
    P:                                              10 Raymund IV BERINGERUS-635-------  on chart no. 8
    M:      1270    --935
    P:                                              This person is the same person 21 o GERSENDA II-638--------
    D:      1309                                    as no. 10 on chart no. 8          Same as no. 21
    P:                                                                                on chart no. 8
                 5 of Provence BEATRIX-1677----------                             22 of Savoy THOMAS I-641----
                   B:      1234                                                      Same as no. 22
                   P:                                                             11 of Savoy BEATRICE-636-----------  on chart no. 8
                   D: 23 Sep 1267                                                              23 o MARGUERITE-642---------
                   P: Nocera                        This person is the same person             Same as no. 23
 1 Princess MARGARET-1582------------                as no. 11 on chart no. 8                   on chart no. 8
    B: Abt    1273                                                                24 K ANDREW II-1591---------
    P: of Naples                                                                     Same as no. 14
    M: 16 Aug 1290   --934                                                        12 King of Hungary BELA IV-1588-----  on chart no. 14
    P: Corbeil                                         B:       1206
    D: 31 Dec 1299                                     P:                          25 of Meran GERTRUDE-1592---
    P:                                                 M:       --937
 Count of Valois CHARLES-1583---                      P:
    Spouse                                            D:      1270/1273
                 6 King of Hungary STEPHEN V-1586----  P:                          26 E LASCARIS I-1590--------
                   B:    Dec 1239/1240
                   P:                               13 Maria LASKARINA-1589------------
                   M:    --936                         B: Abt    1206              27 Anna ANGELINA-1765-------
                   P:                                  P:
                   D: 1 Aug 1272/1273                  D:       1270
                   P:                                  P:                          28 -----------------------
 3 Princess MARIE-1584---------------
    B: Abt    1257                                  14 Prince KUTHEN/ZAYHAN-1678-------
    P: of Hungary                                      B:
    D: 25 Mar 1323                                     P:                          29 -----------------------
    P:                                                 M:       --987
                                                      P:
                                                      D:
                 7 of Kumans ELIZABETH-1587----------  P:                          30 -----------------------
                   B:
                   P:
                   D: Aft    1290                   15 -----------------------
                   P:                                  B:                          31 -----------------------
                                                      P:
                                                      D:
                                                      P:
```

The Spear and the Spindle:
Ancestors of Sir Francis Bryan (d. 1550)
Bryan, Bourchier, Bohun, FitzAlan, and Others   **Genealogical Table**

.Chart No. 20

Number 1 on this chart is the same as no. 24 on chart no. 4

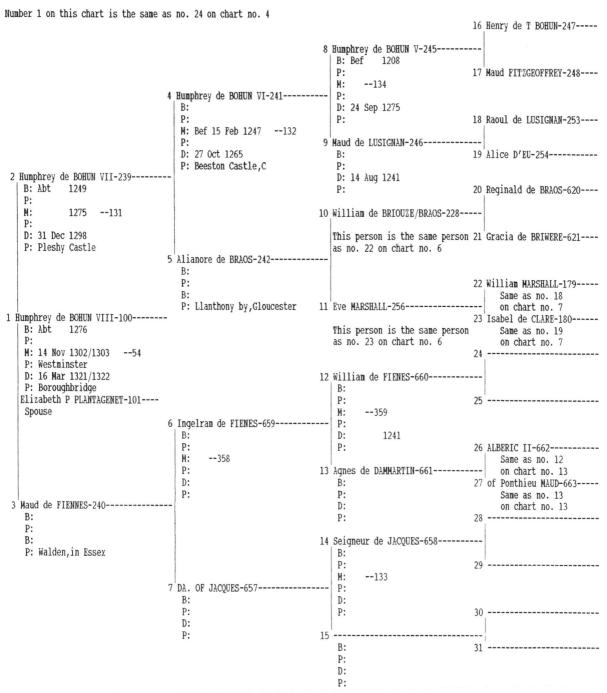

```
                                                                        16 Henry de T BOHUN-247-----

                                               8 Humphrey de BOHUN V-245----------
                                                  B: Bef    1208
                                                  P:                                17 Maud FITZGEOFFREY-248----
                                                  M:    --134
                        4 Humphrey de BOHUN VI-241----------  P:
                          B:                                  D: 24 Sep 1275
                          P:                                  P:                    18 Raoul de LUSIGNAN-253----
                          M: Bef 15 Feb 1247   --132
                          P:                               9 Maud de LUSIGNAN-246-------------
                          D: 27 Oct 1265                     B:                     19 Alice D'EU-254-----------
                          P: Beeston Castle,C                P:
                                                             D: 14 Aug 1241
 2 Humphrey de BOHUN VII-239---------                        P:                    20 Reginald de BRAOS-620----
   B: Abt    1249
   P:
   M:       1275   --131                               10 William de BRIOUZE/BRAOS-228-----
   P:
   D: 31 Dec 1298                                         This person is the same person  21 Gracia de BRIWERE-621----
   P: Pleshy Castle                                       as no. 22 on chart no. 6
                        5 Alianore de BRAOS-242-------------
                          B:
                          P:                                                       22 William MARSHALL-179-----
                          B:                                                          Same as no. 18
                          P: Llanthony by,Gloucester    11 Eve MARSHALL-256----------------|  on chart no. 7
 1 Humphrey de BOHUN VIII-100-------                                               23 Isabel de CLARE-180------
   B: Abt    1276                                         This person is the same person     Same as no. 19
   P:                                                     as no. 23 on chart no. 6           on chart no. 7
   M: 14 Nov 1302/1303   --54                                                      24 ------------------------
   P: Westminster
   D: 16 Mar 1321/1322                                  12 William de FIENES-660-----------
   P: Boroughbridge                                        B:
   Elizabeth P PLANTAGENET-101----                         P:                      25 ------------------------
   Spouse                                                  M:    --359
                        6 Ingelram de FIENES-659------------  P:
                          B:                                D:       1241
                          P:                                P:                      26 ALBERIC II-662-----------
                          M:    --358                                                  Same as no. 12
                          P:                             13 Agnes de DAMMARTIN-661-----------  on chart no. 13
                          D:                                B:                      27 of Ponthieu MAUD-663-----
                          P:                                P:                         Same as no. 13
 3 Maud de FIENNES-240--------------                        D:                         on chart no. 13
   B:                                                       P:                      28 ------------------------
   P:
   B:                                                   14 Seigneur de JACQUES-658----------
   P: Walden,in Essex                                      B:
                                                           P:                      29 ------------------------
                                                           M:    --133
                        7 DA. OF JACQUES-657----------------  P:
                          B:                                D:
                          P:                                P:                      30 ------------------------
                          D:
                          P:                            15 ------------------------------
                                                           B:                      31 ------------------------
                                                           P:
                                                           D:
                                                           P:
```

The Spear and the Spindle:
Ancestors of Sir Francis Bryan (d. 1550)
Bryan, Bourchier, Bohun, FitzAlan, and Others

Genealogical Table

Number 1 on this chart is the same as no. 25 on chart no. 4

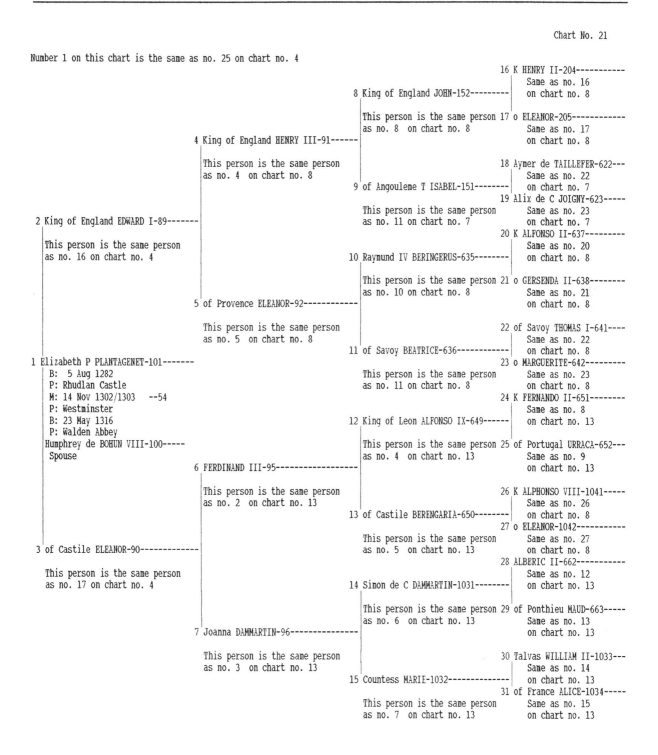

16 K HENRY II-204-----------
   Same as no. 16
   on chart no. 8

8 King of England JOHN-152---------

This person is the same person   17 o ELEANOR-205------------
as no. 8 on chart no. 8   Same as no. 17
                                     on chart no. 8

4 King of England HENRY III-91------

This person is the same person   18 Aymer de TAILLEFER-622---
as no. 4 on chart no. 8   Same as no. 22
                                        on chart no. 7

9 of Angouleme T ISABEL-151-------   19 Alix de C JOIGNY-623-----
                                         Same as no. 23
This person is the same person   on chart no. 7
as no. 11 on chart no. 7

                                      20 K ALFONSO II-637---------
                                         Same as no. 20
10 Raymund IV BERINGERUS-635-------   on chart no. 8

2 King of England EDWARD I-89-------

This person is the same person   This person is the same person 21 o GERSENDA II-638--------
as no. 16 on chart no. 4   as no. 10 on chart no. 8   Same as no. 21
                                                                       on chart no. 8

5 of Provence ELEANOR-92------------

This person is the same person   22 of Savoy THOMAS I-641----
as no. 5 on chart no. 8   Same as no. 22
                                         on chart no. 8

11 of Savoy BEATRICE-636------------ 23 o MARGUERITE-642---------
                                         Same as no. 23
1 Elizabeth P PLANTAGENET-101------- This person is the same person on chart no. 8
   B: 5 Aug 1282   as no. 11 on chart no. 8
   P: Rhudlan Castle   24 K FERNANDO II-651--------
   M: 14 Nov 1302/1303   --54   Same as no. 8
   P: Westminster   on chart no. 13
   B: 23 May 1316   12 King of Leon ALFONSO IX-649------
   P: Walden Abbey
   Humphrey de BOHUN VIII-100-----   This person is the same person 25 of Portugal URRACA-652---
   Spouse   as no. 4 on chart no. 13   Same as no. 9
                                                                       on chart no. 13

6 FERDINAND III-95-----------------

This person is the same person   26 K ALPHONSO VIII-1041-----
as no. 2 on chart no. 13   Same as no. 26
                                         on chart no. 8

13 of Castile BERENGARIA-650-------   27 o ELEANOR-1042-----------
                                         Same as no. 27
This person is the same person   on chart no. 8
as no. 5 on chart no. 13

3 of Castile ELEANOR-90------------- 28 ALBERIC II-662-----------
                                         Same as no. 12
This person is the same person   on chart no. 13
as no. 17 on chart no. 4

14 Simon de C DAMMARTIN-1031-------

This person is the same person 29 of Ponthieu MAUD-663-----
as no. 6 on chart no. 13   Same as no. 13
                                  on chart no. 13

7 Joanna DAMMARTIN-96--------------

This person is the same person   30 Talvas WILLIAM II-1033---
as no. 3 on chart no. 13   Same as no. 14
                                         on chart no. 13

15 Countess MARIE-1032-------------   31 of France ALICE-1034-----
                                         Same as no. 15
This person is the same person   on chart no. 13
as no. 7 on chart no. 13

31

The Spear and the Spindle:
Ancestors of Sir Francis Bryan (d. 1550)
Bryan, Bourchier, Bohun, FitzAlan, and Others

Genealogical Table

Chart No. 22

Number 1 on this chart is the same as no. 26 on chart no. 4

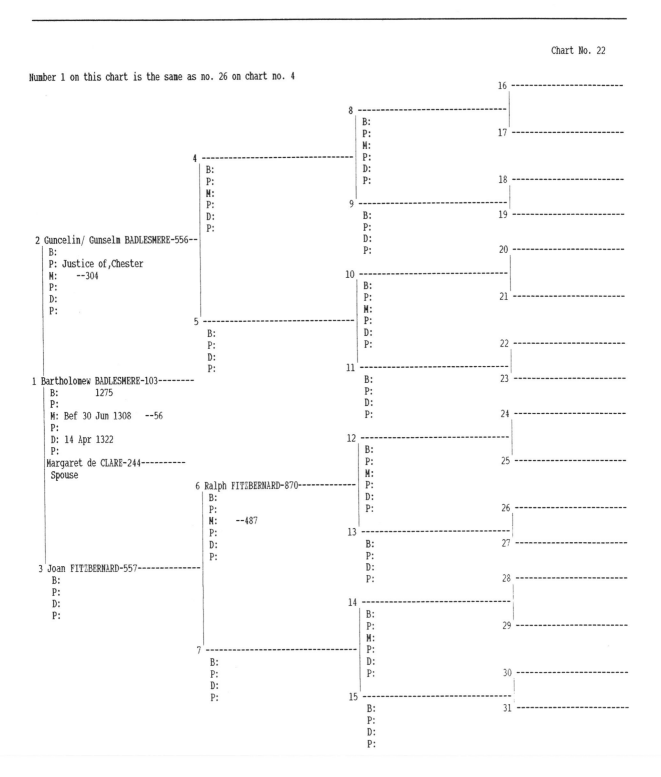

```
                                                                    16 -------------------------
                                                   8 -----------------------------
                                                    B:
                                                    P:                          17 -------------------------
                                                    M:
                         4 ---------------------------    P:
                          B:                             D:
                          P:                             P:                      18 -------------------------
                          M:
                          P:                        9 -----------------------------
                          D:                         B:                          19 -------------------------
                          P:                         P:
                                                     D:
 2 Guncelin/ Gunselm BADLESMERE-556--               P:                           20 -------------------------
   B:
   P: Justice of,Chester                           10 -----------------------------
   M:    --304                                       B:
   P:                                                P:                           21 -------------------------
   D:                                                M:
   P:                                                P:
                                                     D:
                         5 ---------------------------    P:                      22 -------------------------
                          B:
                          P:                        11 -----------------------------
                          D:                         B:                          23 -------------------------
                          P:                         P:
 1 Bartholomew BADLESMERE-103--------                D:
   B:      1275                                      P:                           24 -------------------------
   P:
   M: Bef 30 Jun 1308   --56                        12 -----------------------------
   P:                                                B:
   D: 14 Apr 1322                                    P:                           25 -------------------------
   P:                                                M:
 Margaret de CLARE-244----------                    P:
   Spouse                                            D:
                         6 Ralph FITZBERNARD-870-----------    P:                 26 -------------------------
                          B:
                          P:                        13 -----------------------------
                          M:    --487                B:                          27 -------------------------
                          P:                         P:
                          D:                         D:
                          P:                         P:                           28 -------------------------
 3 Joan FITZBERNARD-557--------------
   B:                                               14 -----------------------------
   P:                                                B:
   D:                                                P:                           29 -------------------------
   P:                                                M:
                                                     P:
                         7 -----------------------------    D:
                          B:                             P:                       30 -------------------------
                          P:
                          D:                        15 -----------------------------
                          P:                         B:                          31 -------------------------
                                                     P:
                                                     D:
                                                     P:
```

The Spear and the Spindle:
Ancestors of Sir Francis Bryan (d. 1550)
Bryan, Bourchier, Bohun, FitzAlan, and Others

Genealogical Table

Chart No. 23

Number 1 on this chart is the same as no. 27 on chart no. 4

```
                                                                    16 Richard de T CLARE-362---

                                             8 Gilbert de THE SURETY CLARE-367--
                                               B:
                                               P:                  17 Amice MEULLENT-363-------
                                               M:  9 Oct 1217   --206
                    4 Richard de CLARE-324-------------- P:
                      B:        1222                     D:        1230
                      P:                                 P:        18 William MARSHALL-179-----
                      M:      --183                                   Same as no. 18
                      P:                                              on chart no. 7
                      D:        1262             9 Isabella MARSHALL-368-----------  19 Isabel de CLARE-180------
                      P:                           B:                                  Same as no. 19
                                                   P:                                  on chart no. 7
  2 Thomas de CLARE-322--------------             D:        1240                     20 Roger de LACIE-358-------
    B:                                             P:
    P:                                     10 John de THE SURETY LACIE-356-----
    M:     --182                              B:
    P:                                        P:                   21 Maud de CLARE-359--------
    D:        1286                            M:     --200
    P: Ireland                                P:
                                              D:        1240
                    5 Maud de LACIE-325----------------- P:        22 Robert de QUENCY-366-----
                      B:                                 P:
                      P:                       11 Margaret de QUENCEY-357----------
                      D: Bef    1288             B:                                23 Hawise KEVELIOK-460------
                      P:                         P:
  1 Margaret de CLARE-244-------------           D:        1266
    B:                                           P:        24 G FITZMAURICE-1719-------
    P:
    M: Bef 30 Jun 1308   --56            12 Maurice FITZGERALD-1717----------
    P:                                     B:        1190
    D:        1333                         P:        25 Eve de BERMINGHAM-1720---
    P:                                     M:      --996
  Bartholomew BADLESMERE-103-----          D:        1257
    Spouse                                 P: Youghal            26 ------------------------
                    6 Sir Maurice FITZMAURICE-326------- 
                      B:                          13 Juliane-1718--------------------
                      P:                            B:        27 ------------------------
                      M: Abt    1266   --184        P:
                      P:                            D:
                      D:        1286                P:        28 William LONGESPEE-698----
                      P:
  3 Julian FITZMAURICE-323------------   14 Stephen LONGESPEE-215------------
    B:                                     B:
    P:                                     P:        29 Ela FITZPATRICK-699------
    D:                                     M:      --118
    P:                                     P:
                                           D: Bef 23 Jan 1274/1275
                                           P:                   30 W RIDELISFORD-217--------
                    7 Emmeline de LONGESPEE-1690-------
                      B: Abt    1250       15 Emmeline de RIDELISFORD-216------
                      P:                     B:                31 Annora-1721--------------
                      D:        1291         P:
                      P:                     D:        1276
                                             P:
```

33

The Spear and the Spindle:
Ancestors of Sir Francis Bryan (d. 1550)
Bryan, Bourchier, Bohun, FitzAlan, and Others

Genealogical Table

The Spear and the Spindle:
Ancestors of Sir Francis Bryan (d. 1550)
Bryan, Bourchier, Bohun, FitzAlan, and Others

Short Biographies

Aenor
(d. abt. 1130)(RIN 1609)

Also Eleanor de Chastellerault; mother of Eleanor of Aquitaine; she was about fourteen when married in 1121 to William X "the Toulousain." (Weis, Line 110, says William VIII.)

She had three children by William:
- Eleanor (alia-Aenor, meaning the other Aenor)
- Petronilla (also known as Aelith)
- William Aigret, d. abt 1130 at a young age

Aenor's mother, Dangereuse/Dangerose, was mistress of Duke William IX, the father of Aenor's husband (Aenor was one of three children of Dangereuse's marriage). (Meade, pgs. 7-32)

Alberic II
(d. 1200)(RIN 662) Count of Dammartin. Also Aubry II. Son of Alberic I (RIN 664) (also Aubrey I). Stuart, Line 82, notes that this line has been revised and says that the wife of Alberic I (RIN 664) was Joan Basset of Wellingford, Oxford, England, and that she was "prob mother" of Alberic II; he adds that Alberic I was also married to Clemence de Dammartin, living 1154.

Alfonso II
(d. 1196)(RIN 639) King of Aragon 1163-1196; eldest son of Petronilla, Queen of Aragon. (*KQE*, pg. 38)

Alfonso VII
(d. 1157)(RIN 1038)

King of Castile and Leon; Alphonso-Raimond; reigned 1126-1157; m. (1) Berengaria of Barcelona (RIN 1040) and issue by her included Sancho III (RIN 1043), King of Castile, Fernando II (RIN 651), King of Leon, and Sancha of Castile (RIN 1569) who married Sancho VI (RIN 1568) (NOTE: Stuart, Line 83, notes that some authorities indicate Richilde of Poland (RIN 1039) is mother of Sancho III); Alfonso VII m. (2) Richilda of Poland (RIN 1039) and had Sancha of Castile (RIN 640) who married Alfonso II (RIN 639), King of Aragon.

35

The Spear and the Spindle:
Ancestors of Sir Francis Bryan (d. 1550)
Bryan, Bourchier, Bohun, FitzAlan, and Others   Short Biographies

---

Alfonso VIII
(d. 1214)(RIN 1041)

King of Castile 1158-1214; m. Eleanor of England (RIN 1042). Williamson in *KQE* (pg. 42) states they had four sons and eight daughters.

Alfonso IX, King of Leon
(d. 1229/30)(RIN 649)

Reigned 1188-1230; m. Berengaria, da. of Alfonso VIII (RIN 1041), King of Castile, and Eleanor of England (RIN 1042).

Alice of France
(d.)(RIN 1034)

Half sister of Philip II "Augustus," King of France 1180-1223. She was betrothed to Richard the Lion-Heart, son of Henry II (RIN 204) and Eleanor of Aquitaine (RIN 205), and sent to England at an early age to be reared in the English ways; however, she was never married to Richard but eventually taken as a mistress by Richard's father, Henry II. She later m. William III (RIN 1033), Count of Poitou. Her mother was Alix/Adela/Alice of Champagne (RIN 634), third wife of Louis VII (RIN 633).

```
                                                            K LOUIS VI-761-(b.1077)--------------
                             K LOUIS VII-633-(b.1119)-------------
                                                            o ADELAIDE/ALICE-762-(b.1100)---------
 of France ALICE-1034-(b.1170)---------
                                                            THEOBALD IV-1329---------------------
                             o ALIX/ADELA/ALICE-634-(b.1140)-------
                                                            of Carinthia MATILDA-1441------------
```

Andreas II
(d. 1235)(RIN 1591)

Andrew II; King of Hungary 1205-1235; son of Bela III (RIN 1593) and Anne/Agnes of Chatillon (RIN 1594). M. (1) Gertrude of Meran (d. 1213/1214) (Weis, 6th ed., Line 103); m. (2) Yolande of Courtenay (RIN 1592); m. (3) Beatrix d'Este (d. 1245), who became grandmother of Andrew III, King of Hungary (Previte-Orton, Table 26).

Badlesmere, Elizabeth
(d. 1356)(RIN 99)

M. (1) Edmund Mortimer of Wigmore, Earl of March (b. abt. 1305, d. bef. 21 Jan 1331/32); they were parents of Roger Mortimer (b. 11 Nov 1328 Ludlow, d. 26 Feb 1359 Romera in Burgundy), an original Knight of the Garter, Constable of Dover Castle, Warden of

Short Biographies

The Spear and the Spindle:
Ancestors of Sir Francis Bryan (d. 1550)
Bryan, Bourchier, Bohun, FitzAlan, and Others

Cinque Ports, who m. Philippa Montacute (d. 5 Jan 1381/82), sister of William Montacute (an original Knight of the Garter).

Elizabeth m. (2) Sir William de Bohun (RIN 98), Earl of Northampton. (Weis, 6th ed., Line 65)

Badlesmere, Guncelin
(d.   )(RIN 556)   Justice of Chester.

Baldwin V
(d. 1195)(RIN 597)   Count of Hainaut and Namur; d. 17 Dec 1195, Mons, second husband of Margarite of Lorraine (RIN 598). (Weis, 6th ed., Line 163; Stuart, Line 73)

Baldwin VI
(d. 1205)(RIN 595)   Son of Baldwin V (RIN 597) (d. 17 Dec 1195, Mons), Count of Hainaut and Namur, and Margarite of Lorraine (RIN 598) (d. 15 Nov 1194). Count of Hainaut and Flanders; one of those leading the Fourth Crusade; Emperor of Constantinople. (Weis, 6th ed., Line 168; Stuart, Line 73)

Beatrice
(d.   )(RIN 1727)   Beatrice de Montlucan. Daughter of Archambaud V de Montlucon (RIN 1728).

Beatrix of Savoy
(d.   )(RIN 644)   Beatrix of Macon (Weis, 6th ed., Line 133). Daughter of Thomas I of Savoy (RIN 641) and Marguerite of Foucigny (RIN 642).

Beauchamp, Isabel
(d. abt 1306)(RIN 124)
                    M. (1) Sir Patrick de Chaworth (RIN 110); m. (2) 1286 Sir Hugh le Despenser, Earl of Winchester (b. 1 Mar 1260/61, hanged Oct. 1326), son of Hugh le Despenser and Aline Basset. (*Sureties*)

Beauchamp, William de
(d. abt. 1268)(RIN 231)
                    Lord of Elmley. Son of Walcheline de Beauchamp (RIN 233).

Beauchamp, William de
(d. 1298)(RIN 123)   Baron of Elmley and Earl of Warwick (*MC*, Chapter 249). 9th Earl of Warwick. (*Sureties*)

The Spear and the Spindle:
Ancestors of Sir Francis Bryan (d. 1550)
Bryan, Bourchier, Bohun, FitzAlan, and Others   Short Biographies

```
┌────────────────────────────────────────────────────────────────────────────┐
│                                                  Walcheline de BEAUCHAMP-233----------│
│                              William de BEAUCHAMP-231--------------                  │
│                                                  Joane MORTIMER-234------------------│
│   William de BEAUCHAMP-123-(b.1237)-----                                              │
│                                                  William MAUDIT/MAUDUIT-454-----------│
│                              Isabel MAUDUIT-232-------------------                    │
│                                                  Alice de NEWBURGH-455----------------│
└────────────────────────────────────────────────────────────────────────────┘
```

Bela IV
(d. 1273)(RIN 1588)

King of Hungary 1235-1270. (Weis, 6th ed., Line 103)

Bellomont, Margaret
(d. 1234)(RIN 130) Also spelled Beaumont.

Berengaria of Castile
(d. 1244)(RIN 650) Sister of Blanca (RIN 630) who m. Louis VIII (RIN 629) of France.

Berenguela/Berengaria
(d. 1149)(RIN 1040)

First wife of Alfonso VIII (RIN 1038); widow of Bernard III, Count of
Besalu; her mother Maria Rodriguez de Bivar, was the daughter of
El Cid. (*KQE*, pg. 42)

Beringerus, Margaret
(d. 1295)(RIN 628) Margaret of Provence; bur. St. Denis.

Beringerus, Raymond IV
(d. 1245)(RIN 635) King of Provence. Count of Provence and Forcalquier (Weis, 6th ed.,
Line 111). Son of Alfonso II (RIN 637), King of Provence, and
Gersenda II of Saban (RIN 638).

```
┌────────────────────────────────────────────────────────────────────────────┐
│                                                 ALFONSO II-639-(b.1152)--------------│
│                           King of Provence ALFONSO II-637------                       │
│                                                 of Castile SANCHA-640-(b.1154)--------│
│   Raymund IV BERINGERUS-635-----------                                               │
│                           of Saban GERSENDA II-638------------                        │
│                                                                                      │
└────────────────────────────────────────────────────────────────────────────┘
```

The Spear and the Spindle:
Ancestors of Sir Francis Bryan (d. 1550)
Bryan, Bourchier, Bohun, FitzAlan, and Others

Short Biographies

Berkeley, Maurice
(d. 1326)(RIN 1176)

"The Magnanimous"; Lord Berkeley of Berkeley Castle; his first wife was Eva La Zouche (RIN 1177) (d. 1314); the pair was not over eight years of age when married. (Weis, 6th ed., Line 59)

```
                                                            Maurice de BERKELEY-1712-(b.1218)-----
                            Thomas BERKELEY-1178-----------------
                                                            Isabel FITZROY-1711------------------
Maurice BERKELEY-1176-(b.1271)--------
                                                            William de FERRERS-469-(b.1193)-------
                            Joan FERRERS-1179--------------------
                                                            Margaret de QUINCEY-611--------------
```

Maurice Berkeley was an enemy of the Despensers, the unpopular favorites of Edward II (RIN 87), and he died early in 1326 as their captive. The Despensers had, in effect, pushed Queen Isabelle (RIN 88) aside and taken her place in the affections of Edward II. Queen Isabelle had then taken a lover, Roger Mortimer (RIN 1182), whom she believed could help her not only get rid of the Despensers but remove Edward II from his throne and set up the young Edward (RIN 85) in his place, leaving her to rule as regent. The plan was successful: the Despensers were captured and put to death, and Edward II was taken prisoner.

To offset the number of uprisings aimed at replacing Edward II on the throne, the prisoner had to be moved from castle to castle, and it soon became apparent that Edward II would have to die. He was finally taken to Berkeley Castle, whose Lord was now Thomas of Berkeley (RIN 1174), son of Maurice. It is believed that Isabelle and Mortimer chose Berkeley Castle because Mortimer's daughter, Margaret (RIN 1175), was married to Thomas of Berkeley (RIN 1174).

The men in charge of Edward's imprisonment were Thomas Gurney (a knight), and John Maltravers (RIN 1663), who was married to Thomas's sister, Milicent/Ela Berkeley (RIN 1662). It is evident that Thomas of Berkeley did not welcome this situation: having shown kindness to his royal prisoner, he was no longer allowed to see Edward. In September of 1327, a fourth man, William Ogle, arrived at Berkeley. Gurney, Maltravers, and Ogle now had charge of the prisoner. Thomas, fearing the worst and knowing he could not change the matter, left his castle. On the night of 21 September, Edward II was cruelly put to death. (Costain, *The Three Edwards*; Oman, Berkeley section)

The Spear and the Spindle:
Ancestors of Sir Francis Bryan (d. 1550)
Bryan, Bourchier, Bohun, FitzAlan, and Others   Short Biographies

---

Berkeley, Maurice de
(d. 1281)(RIN 1712)

6th Lord Berkeley. (Weis, 6th ed., Line 26)

Berkeley, Milicent de (Ela)
(d. aft 1322)(RIN 1662)

John Maltravers (RIN 1663) was her first husband (Weis, 6th ed., Line 59) and was probably one of the men who murdered Edward II (RIN 85); see under Maurice Berkeley (RIN 1176).

Berkeley, Thomas
(d.   )(RIN 1174)   Lord of Berkeley; "the Ritch"; Thomas of Berkeley; married to the daughter of Roger Mortimer (RIN 1182), lover of Edward II's (RIN 87) queen, Isabelle (RIN 88). For the part Thomas of Berkeley did *not* play in the murder of Edward II, see under his father, Maurice Berkeley (RIN 1176).

Berkeley, Sir Thomas
(d. 1321)(RIN 1178)

"The Wise"; his great-grandfather was John (RIN 152), King of England. (Weis, 6th ed., Line 59)

Bermingham, Eve de
(d. 1226)(RIN 1720)

Daughter and heir of Robert de Bermingham; m. (1) Gerald FitzMaurice (RIN 1719); m. (2) Geoffrey FitzRobert, baron of Kells; m. (3) Geoffrey de Marisco. (Weis, 6th ed., Line 178)

Bigod, Hugh
(d. 1225)(RIN 177)   Surety for the Magna Charta; Earl of Norfolk and Suffolk (*MC,* Chapter 249). Son of Roger Bigod (RIN 202), Earl of Norfolk (d. 1220), who was also a Surety for the Magna Charta.

Bigod, Isabel
(d.   )(RIN 176)   Her marriage to John FitzGeoffrey (RIN 175) was her second marriage (*MC,* Chapter 249). She was the daughter of Hugh Bigod (RIN 177), the Magna Charta Surety, and Maud Marshall (RIN 178).

The Spear and the Spindle:
Ancestors of Sir Francis Bryan (d. 1550)
Bryan, Bourchier, Bohun, FitzAlan, and Others

Short Biographies

Blanche of Artois

(d. 1302)(RIN 127) Queen of Navarre; second wife of Edmund (RIN 126), Earl of Lancaster (*MC*, Part IV). Widow of Henry I (RIN 1444), King of Navarre.

```
                                                         K LOUIS VIII-629-(b.1187)------------
                              ROBERT-129-(b.1216)-----------------
                                                         of Castile BLANCHE-630-(b.1188)-------
       of Artois BLANCHE-127---------------
                                                         HENRY II-1510-----------------------
                              of Brabant MATILDA-213--------------
                                                         of Germany MARY-1509-----------------
```

Blanche of Castile

(d. 1252)(RIN 630) Queen Regent of France 1226-1234; founded the Abbey of Maubuisson where she was buried. Daughter of Alphonso VIII (RIN 1041) and Eleanor of England (RIN 1042).

Blanche of Navarre

(d. 1229)(RIN 1556)

Princess of Navarre; daughter of Sancho VI (RIN 1568), King of Navarre (d. 1194, Pamplona), and Sancha of Castile (RIN 1569) (m. 20 Jul 1153, d. 5 Aug 1177). (Stuart, Line 86)

Bohun, Eleanor

(d. 1399)(RIN 1612)

Wife of Thomas of Woodstock (RIN 1611) and elder daughter and co-heir of Humphrey Bohun IX (RIN 1615), Earl of Hereford, Essex, and Northampton. Her husband was styled Earl of Essex in her right.

```
                                                         William BOHUN-98-(b.1310)------------
                              Humphrey BOHUN IX-1615----------------
                                                         Elizabeth BADLESMERE-99-(b.1313)------
       Alianore/Eleanor BOHUN-1612----------
                                                         Richard II FITZALAN-104-(b.1313)------
                              Joan FITZALAN-1616-------------------
                                                         of Lancaster ELEANOR-105-------------
```

Their children were:
- Humphrey, Earl of Buckingham (b. abt 1381, d. abt 1399). Humphrey was a "guest" of Richard II, being held to assure the

The Spear and the Spindle:
Ancestors of Sir Francis Bryan (d. 1550)
Bryan, Bourchier, Bohun, FitzAlan, and Others   Short Biographies

good behavior of his father at the time of Henry of Bolingbrook's move to depose Richard. With Humphrey was Henry, son of Bolingbrook and the future Henry V. Humphrey died soon after Richard was deposed, either by illness or shipwreck. He was buried in Walden Abbey, Essex.

- Anne Plantagenet (RIN 1613)
- Joan, betrothed to Gilbert, Lord Talbot, but died unmarried 16 Aug 1400
- Isabel became a nun
- Philippa (d. young)

Eleanor died 9 Aug 1399 from grief, it was said, at the loss of her son (*D.N.B.*, "Thomas of Woodstock"). She was buried near her husband, in the Chapel of St. Edmund in Westminster Abbey. (*Westminster Abbey: Official Guide*)

Bohun, Henry de
(d. 1220)(RIN 247)   Sheriff of Kent; 5th Earl of Hereford; Magna Charta Surety; died while on pilgrimage to the Holy Land (Weis, 6th ed., Line 7). *D.N.B.* says 1st Earl of Hereford; b. 1176; created Earl of Hereford 1176; supported Louis of France during the poor rule of King John. (*D.N.B.*, "Henry de Bohun")

Bohun, Humphrey V de
(d. 1275)(RIN 245)   2nd Earl of Hereford; 1st Earl of Essex; Constable of England; Sheriff of Kent; in 1236 he was marshall of the household at the coronation of Henry III's queen, Eleanor; he was one of the sponsors at the christening of Prince Edward (RIN 89) (to be Edward I of England); he m. (1) Maud, daughter of the count of Eu, and had Humphrey VI (RIN 241) and four daughters; he m. (2) Maud de Avenebury and had a son John, Lord of Haresfield. (Weis, 6th ed., Line 97; *D.N.B.*, "Humphrey V de Bohun")

Bohun, Humphrey VI de
(d. 1265)(RIN 241)   Died before his father; *D.N.B.* says Humphrey died 27 Aug 1265, after the Battle of Evesham where he was captured fighting for Simon de Montfort. Died at Beeston Castle, co. Chester. (*D.N.B.*, "Humphrey VII de Bohun")

Short Biographies

The Spear and the Spindle:
Ancestors of Sir Francis Bryan (d. 1550)
Bryan, Bourchier, Bohun, FitzAlan, and Others

```
                                                          Henry de T BOHUN-247-(b.1176)---------
                            Humphrey de BOHUN V-245-(b.1208)------
                                                          Maud FITZGEOFFREY-248----------------
  Humphrey de BOHUN VI-241-------------
                                                          Raoul de LUSIGNAN-253----------------
                            Maud de LUSIGNAN-246----------------
                                                          Alice D'EU-254-(b.1246)--------------
```

Bohun, Humphrey VII de

(d. 1298)(RIN 239)   3rd Earl of Hereford and 2nd Earl of Essex; Constable of England; in 1276/77 he was sent to escort home John, the Earl of Holland, and his wife, the Princess Elizabeth (RIN 101); at that time the princess was fourteen years old; two years later she, as a widow, married Humphrey's son, Humphrey VIII de Bohun (RIN 100); Humphrey VII died at Pleshy Castle and was buried at Walden in Essex. (*CP*, Essex section; Weis, 6th ed., Line 97; *D.N.B.*, "Humphrey VII de Bohun")

Bohun, Humphrey VIII de

(d. 1322)(RIN 100)   Born 1276; 4th Earl of Hereford and 3rd Earl of Essex; constable of England. He m. 1302 Elizabeth (RIN 101), daughter of Edward I (RIN 89), widow of John, Earl of Holland.

He fought against Robert Bruce. He was one of the ordainers to reform Edward II's government and household and banish Edward's favorite, Piers Gaveston, from the country. The king later recalled Gaveston, and Hereford was among the group that captured and beheaded the favorite at Blacklow Hill. Edward could not punish the men and later pardoned them.

Humphrey was taken prisoner at the Battle of Bannockburn and exchanged for the wife of Robert Bruce (she had been a captive in England).

When the Despensers took the place of Gaveston in Edward's affections, the Lords rebelled; however, Edward took arms against them in the Battle of Boroughbridge in Yorkshire on 16 Mar 1322, and Humphrey was among those killed. He was buried in the church of the Friars Preachers of York.

Humphrey and the Princess Elizabeth had six sons and four daughters. His second son, John (d. 1335), succeeded him; John was succeeded by

The Spear and the Spindle:
Ancestors of Sir Francis Bryan (d. 1550)
Bryan, Bourchier, Bohun, FitzAlan, and Others   Short Biographies

his brother, Humphrey IX (RIN 1615) (d. 1361). (Ross, pg. 183; Weis, 6th ed., Line 97; *D.N.B.*, "Humphrey VIII de Bohun")

Bohun, Humphrey IX de
(d. 1372)(RIN 1615)

Earl of Hereford, Essex, and Northampton.

```
                                                        Humphrey de BOHUN VIII-100-(b.1276)---
                            William BOHUN-98-(b.1310)-----------
                                                        Elizabeth P PLANTAGENET-101-(b.1282)--
        Humphrey BOHUN IX-1615--------------
                                                        Bartholomew BADLESMERE-103-(b.1275)---
                            Elizabeth BADLESMERE-99-(b.1313)-----
                                                        Margaret de CLARE-244----------------
```

Bohun, William
(d. 1360)(RIN 98)   Earl of Northampton; 4th Earl of Hereford; fifth son of Humphrey de Bohun VIII (RIN 100); born abt 1310; created Earl of Northampton 1337; governor of Ooughmaben Castle in Dumfriesshire, Scotland; his wife, Elizabeth Badlesmere (RIN 99) was widow of Edmund Mortimer; upon his death, his son, Humphrey IX (RIN 1615), succeeded him. William died 16 Sep 1360 and was buried at Walden in Essex (*D.N.B.*, "William de Bohun").

Botiller, Maud
(d. 1283)(RIN 156)   Daughter of Theobald le Botiller (RIN 165) and Rohese de Verdun (RIN 166).

Bourbon, Archambaud IX de
(d. 1242)(RIN 665)   Died in Battle of Taillebourg; son of Gui II de Bourbon (RIN 1729) (d. 18 Jan 1216) and Matilda de Bourbon (RIN 1730) (b. abt 1165, d. 18 Jun 1228). (Stuart, Line 84)

Bourchier, Sir Humphrey
(d. 1471)(RIN 1619)
                      Knight; son of Sir John Bourchier (RIN 1617), 1st Baron Berners. Sir Humphrey was killed at the Battle of Barnet while fighting for Edward IV. This Sir Humphrey had a daughter Margaret Bourchier (RIN 1624) and a son John Bourchier (d. Calais abt 19 Mar 1532/33) who became 2nd Baron Berners. John, 2nd Lord Berners, m. Katherine Howard (d. 12 Mar 1535-37). Katherine was the daughter of Sir John Howard (slain and attainted 1485) (*CP*, Norfolk table), Duke of Norfolk, and

Margaret Wyfold Norreys, the daughter of Sir John Chedworth;
Katherine was also half-sister of Sir Thomas Howard (d. 1524),
2nd Duke of Norfolk, and father of Anne Boleyn's mother (Weis,
6th ed., Lines 4, 16). Buried in the Chapel of St. Edmund, Westminster
Abbey. (*Westminster Abbey: Official Guide*, pgs. 82, 83)

```
                                                               Sir William BOURCHIER-1614-----------
                                  Sir John BOURCHIER-1617-------------
                                                               Anne PLANTAGENET-1613-(b.1380)--------
Sir Humphrey BOURCHIER-1619---------
                                                               Sir Richard BERNERS-1628-------------
                                  Margery BERNERS-1618----------------
                                                               Philippa DALYNGRIDGE-1629------------
```

Bourchier, Sir John
(d. 1474)(RIN 1617)

Lord Berners; youngest son (*D.N.B.*, "Bourchier"; *CP*, Essex section);
created 1st Baron Berners in 1455; K.G. abt 23 Apr 1459; Constable of
Windsor Castle 1461-1474 (Weis, 6th ed., Line 4). For a list of his
siblings, see his father, Sir William Bourchier (RIN 1614).

John Bourchier was chamberlain to Edward IV's queen, Elizabeth
Woodville; his wife, Margery Berners (RIN 1618), was the constant
attendant of Edward's daughter, the Princess Elizabeth; and his son
Humphrey (RIN 1619) was one of the Queen consort's carvers. (Clive,
pg. 115; Hicks, pg. 35)

Bourchier, Margaret
(d. 1551/52)(RIN 1624)

Daughter of Elizabeth Tylney by her first husband, Humphrey Bourchier
(RIN 1619); half-sister of Queen Anne Boleyn's mother; Lady Bryan;
nurse to Henry VIII's children (Queen) Mary, (Queen) Elizabeth, and
Edward VI; it was this Lady Bryan with whom Queen Anne Boleyn
corresponded concerning the young Princesses. (Ives, 1986)

The Spear and the Spindle:
Ancestors of Sir Francis Bryan (d. 1550)
Bryan, Bourchier, Bohun, FitzAlan, and Others

Short Biographies

```
                                                              Sir John BOURCHIER-1617--------------
                                      Sir Humphrey BOURCHIER-1619---------
                                                              Margery BERNERS-1618----------------
        Margaret "Lady Bryan" BOURCHIER-1624-
                                                              Sir Frederick TYLNEY-1621------------
                                      Elizabeth TYLNEY-1620---------------
                                                              Elizabeth CHENEY-1622----------------
```

Bourchier, Sir William
(d. 1420)(RIN 1614)

Earl of Ewe/Eu; Count of Ewe/Eu; third husband of Anne Plantagenet (RIN 1613), Countess of Buckingham and daughter of Thomas of Woodstock (RIN 1611). (*D.N.B.*, "Bourchier"; *CP*, Essex section)

Their sons were:
- Henry Bourchier (d. 4 Apr 1483, Battle of Barnet), Viscount Bourchier, Earl of Essex; his son was Humphrey Bourchier, Lord Cromwell
- Thomas Bourchier, Archbishop of Canterbury
- William, Lord Fitzwarin, third son and ancestor of the earls of Bath
- John Bourchier, Lord Berners (RIN 1617); great-grandfather of Sir Francis Bryan (RIN 1626).

(*CP*, Essex section)

Bowsey, Sir John
(d.   )(RIN 1644)   Lord Barnes.

Briouze, Maud de
(d. bef 23 Mar 1300/01)(RIN 227)

Maud of Brecknock; daughter of William de Briouze/Braos (RIN 228) and Eve Marshall (RIN 256).

Briouze/Braos, William de
(d.   )(RIN 228)   William of Brecknock and of Abergavenny. A descendant of Griffith Ap Llewellyn Prince of North Wales (slain 5 Aug 1063). (Weis, 6th ed., Line 177)

Brun, Alice/Alix le
(d.   )(RIN 120)   Alice de Lusignan.

The Spear and the Spindle:
Ancestors of Sir Francis Bryan (d. 1550)
Bryan, Bourchier, Bohun, FitzAlan, and Others

Short Biographies

Brun, Hugh
(d.   )(RIN 150)   Count of Marche. Son of Hugh IX de Lusignan (RIN 1389) and Matilda (RIN 1390).

Bryan, Edmund
(d.   )(RIN 1647)   Son of Thomas Bryan (RIN 1650) and Margaret Echyngham (RIN 1651).

Bryan, Sir Francis
(d. 1550)(RIN 1626)

Knight Banneret; Chevallier; Baronet; Lord of Tor Bryan; poet and translator; chief gentleman of the privy chamber (appointed 1536) and close friend of Henry VIII; he was a sometime commander of the English Army in Ireland, admiral of the fleet, and in 1548 was Governor General of Ireland; (MacKenzie, Vol. II, pg. 151, 1966). He was knighted for bravery in Brittany (*Brianiana*). On Shrove Tuesday 1526, he lost an eye in a jousting tournament (Starkey, David, *Henry VIII, A European Court in England*, Cross River Press, NY, 1991, pg. 47).

```
┌─────────────────────────────────────────────────────────────────────────────┐
│                                                  Sir Thomas BRYAN-1631--------------- │
│                          Sir Thomas BRYAN-1625---------------                  │
│                                                  Margaret BOWSEY-1643--------------- │
│  Sir Francis BRYAN-1626-(b.1490)------                                         │
│                                                  Sir Humphrey BOURCHIER-1619---------- │
│                          Margaret "Lady Bryan" BOURCHIER-1624-                 │
│                                                  Elizabeth TYLNEY-1620--------------- │
└─────────────────────────────────────────────────────────────────────────────┘
```

His sister Elizabeth m. Nicholas Carewe, Kt., who was executed in 1539; his sister Margaret (d. by 1521) m. Henry Guildford, Kt. (d. 1532).

Bryan m. (1) after 1517 Philippa (RIN 1627) (d. aft 1534), widow of Sir John Fortescue [*D.N.B.*, "Sir Francis Bryan (d. 1550)"] and daughter of Sir John Montgomery of Scotland (MacKenzie, Vol. II, pg. 151); by this marriage he came into the possession of Faulkbourne Hall (Addison, pg. 31); m. (2) bef Aug 1548 (*CP*, Ormond section) Joan Fitzgerald, daughter of James Fitzgerald, Earl of Desmond. Joan was countess and dowager of Ormond.

Bryan was present with Henry VIII in 1520 at the Field of Cloth of Gold. In 1528, Henry sent Bryan to Rome to obtain papal sanction for

The Spear and the Spindle:
Ancestors of Sir Francis Bryan (d. 1550)
Bryan, Bourchier, Bohun, FitzAlan, and Others   **Short Biographies**

___

his divorce from his queen, Catherine of Aragon, in order that he might marry Anne Boleyn. The mission, of course, failed.

During Henry's courtship of Anne Boleyn, Bryan was an advocate of his rising "cousin," as he called her (see Appendix A). He was of the group (including Harry Norris, Francis Weston, William Brereton, Thomas Wyatt, Edward Seymour, and George Boleyn, brother of Queen Anne Boleyn) that had its center in Anne Boleyn. Henry VIII's lasting affection for Bryan and Bryan's own sense of self preservation protected him during the time of downfall of Henry's second queen; while others literally lost their heads because of Henry's determination to rid himself of Anne, Bryan came through unscathed.

He was present 15 Oct 1537 for the christening of Prince Edward, Henry's son by Jane Seymour and afterwards Edward VI. He was among the group that met Henry's fourth wife, Anne of Cleves, at Calais and escorted her into England. He was a member of parliament for Buckinghamshire in 1542 and 1544, and in Feb 1547 at the funeral of Henry VIII [*D.N.B.*, "Sir Francis Bryan (d. 1550)"] took chief place as "master of the henchmen" (attendants) (*Brianiana*).

Bef 28 Aug 1548, Bryan m. Joan, daughter of James FitzMaurice (FitzGerald), 10th earl of Desmond (*CP*, Ormond section). This was a political marriage intended to prevent Joan from marrying with Gerald FitzGerald, the heir of the 15th Earl of Desmond, a marriage that would have united two chief Irish noble houses. Bryan became Lord Marshal of Ireland and in the following year was elected Lord Justice. Two months later, on 2 Feb 1550, Bryan died suddenly at Clonmel. An autopsy was performed, but the cause of death was not discovered. Within a year, Joan married Gerald [*D.N.B.*, "Sir Francis Bryan (d. 1550)"]; Berleth, 1978; *CP*, Desmond section, Ormond section). Bur. Waterford (*Brianiana*). See also Appendix B.

Bryan, Sir Thomas
(d. 1500)(RIN 1631)

Grandfather of Sir Francis Bryan; Chief Justice of the Common Pleas 1471-1550 (*D.N.B.*); "believed to have been" a descendant of Sir Guy de Bryan (d. 1390) of Walwyn's Castlen (*Brianiana*). See Appendix B for information concerning Sir Guy de Bryan.

Bryan, Sir William de
(d. 1413)(RIN 1652)

First husband of Joan FitzAlan (RIN 1653).

Short Biographies

The Spear and the Spindle:
Ancestors of Sir Francis Bryan (d. 1550)
Bryan, Bourchier, Bohun, FitzAlan, and Others

Bures, Alice

(d.)(RIN 1648)　　　Daughter of Sir Robert de Bures (RIN 1649).

Cantilupe, Milicant de

(d. 1299)(RIN 1181)

Also Cantelou or Cauntelo. (Weis, 6th ed., Line 66)

Cantilupe, William de

(d. 1254)(RIN 1186)

Baron Abergavenny (Weis, 6th ed., Line 66). Son of William. Cantilupe (RIN 1716).

Charles

(d. 1325)(RIN 1583)

Son of Philip III, King of France. (*MC*, pg. 430)

Charles I

(d. 1285)(RIN 1676)

Count of Anjou, King of Naples, Sicily, and Jerusalem; son of Louis VIII (RIN 629), King of France (Weis, 6th ed., Line 104; Stuart, Line 88). Brother of Louis IX (RIN 255) and Robert I (RIN 129), from whom grew the house of Artois (de Castries, Table "The Direct Capetians").

```
                                                          K PHILIP II-631-(b.1165)-------------
                              K LOUIS VIII-629-(b.1187)-----------
                                                          of Hainault ISABELLA-632-(b.1170)-----
        CHARLES I-1676-(b.1220)-------------
                                                          ALPHONSO VIII-1041------------------
                              of Castile BLANCHE-630-(b.1188)------
                                                          of England ELEANOR-1042-(b.1162)------
```

Charles II

(d. 1309)(RIN 1585)

King of Naples (Weis, 6th ed., Line 104). Brother of Philip IV (RIN 579), King of France. From him grew the house of Valois and Alencon (de Castries, Table "The Direct Capetians").

The Spear and the Spindle:
Ancestors of Sir Francis Bryan (d. 1550)
Bryan, Bourchier, Bohun, FitzAlan, and Others   Short Biographies

Chaworth, Maud

(d. bef. 3 Dec 1322)(RIN 109)

> M. (1) Sir Patrick de Chaworth (RIN 110); m. (2) Hugh Despenser, Earl of Winchester, who was hanged Oct. 1326. She was buried Mottisfont Priory.

Chaworth, Sir Patrick de

(d. 1282)(RIN 110) Lord of Kidwelly, Wales, and son of Patrick de Chaworth (*Sureties*). Of Kidwelly Co., Carmarthan. (*MC*, Part IV)

Cheney, Elizabeth

(d.   )(RIN 1622) Daughter of Lawrence Cheney, Esq. (RIN 1623), and wife of Sir Frederick Tylney (RIN 1621) of Boston co., Lincs. (*Sureties*, Line 18). [For reference and future research: an Elizabeth Cheyne (not necessarily this RIN 1622), daughter of Lawrence Cheyne, of Ditton, co. Cambridge, m. Sir John de Saye. They were parents of Anne, who m. (1) 20 Feb 1484 Sir Henry Wentworth, Lord le Despenser (d. between 17 Aug 1499 and 27 Feb 1500/01). (*Sureties*, Line 37)]

Clare, Gilbert de

(d. 1230)(RIN 367) Surety for the Magna Charta; son of Richard de Clare (RIN 362) (d. 1217), Earl of Hereford, also a Surety for the Magna Charta. First husband of Isabella Marshall (RIN 368).

Clare, Isabel Fitz Gilbert

(d. 1220)(RIN 180) Countess of Pembroke; wife of William Marshall, "The Protector" (RIN 179). (*MC*, pg. 773; Duby, pgs. 8, 136)

They had five sons and five daughters (all five sons died issueless):
- William, 2nd Earl of Pembroke (d. 1231)
- Richard, 3rd Earl of Pembroke (d. 1234)
- Gilbert, 4th Earl of Pembroke (d. 1241)
- Walter, 5th Earl of Pembroke (d. 1245)
- Anselm, 6th Earl, but d. 23 Dec 1245 before his investiture as Earl of Pembroke
- Matilda/Maud (RIN 178) (d. 1248) m. (1) 1206 Hugh Bigod (RIN 177), 3rd Earl of Norfolk and a Surety for the Magna Charta, and had Roger; m. (2) William Plantagenet de Warren (RIN 181) (d. 1240)
- Isabella m. (1) 1217 Gilbert de Clare (RIN 367), 7th Earl of Clare and a Surety for the Magna Charta, and had six children; she m. (2) 1231 Richard of Cornwall

Short Biographies

The Spear and the Spindle:
Ancestors of Sir Francis Bryan (d. 1550)
Bryan, Bourchier, Bohun, FitzAlan, and Others

- Sibilla (RIN 470) m. William (RIN 469), Earl of Ferrers/Derby, and had seven daughters
- Eva (RIN 256) m. William (RIN 228), son of Reginald de Braose (RIN 620), and had a daughter Matilda (RIN 227) who m. Roger Mortimer (RIN 226) (d. 1282)
- Johanna m. Warin de Munchensi and had John and Johanna who m. William de Valence, Earl of Pembroke

Isabel was buried at Tintern, Monmouthshire. (*D.N.B.*, "William Marshal")

Clare, Margaret de
(d. 1333)(RIN 244) M. (1) 1289 Gilbert de Umfraville, Earl of Angus (dead in 1303); m. (2) Bartholomew de Badlesmere (RIN 103), who was hanged in 1322. (Weis, 6th ed., Line 54)

Clare, Richare de
(d. 1262)(RIN 324) Earl of Gloucester and Hertford (*MC*, Part IV). His daughter Rohese (by his second wife, Maud de Lacy), m. 1270 Roger de Mowbray (d. bef. 21 Nov 1297). (*CP*, Vol. IX, Mowbray section)

```
                                                             Richard de THE SURETY CLARE-362-------
                                 Gilbert de THE SURETY CLARE-367------
                                                             Amice MEULLENT-363--------------------
  Richard de CLARE-324-(b.1222)--------
                                                             William MARSHALL-179-(b.1153)---------
                                 Isabella MARSHALL-368---------------
                                                             Isabel de CLARE-180-(b.1173)----------
```

Clare, Richard de
(d. 1217)(RIN 362) Surety for the Magna Charta; Earl of Hereford; father of Gilbert de Clare (RIN 367) (d. 1230), also a Surety for the Magna Charta.

Clare, Thomas de
(d. 1286)(RIN 322) Governor of London, Lord of Inchequin and Youghae.

Colchester, Helen de
(d. 1249)(RIN 1637)

Daughter of Walter de Colchester (RIN 1638) and Joan Manchesne (RIN 1639).

The Spear and the Spindle:
Ancestors of Sir Francis Bryan (d. 1550)
Bryan, Bourchier, Bohun, FitzAlan, and Others   Short Biographies

---

D'Aubigny, Isabel
(d.   )(RIN 158)   Her great-grandmother, Adeliza of Louvain (RIN 173) (d. 1151), was
the second wife of Henry I of England (there was no issue of Henry I's
second marriage).

D'Avesnes, Bouchard
(d. abt 1243)(RIN 593)
Archdeacon of Laon and Canon of St. Pierre de Lille; second husband
of Margaret (RIN 594). (Weis, 6th ed., Line 168)

D'Avesnes, Jacques
(d. 1191)(RIN 1731)
Seigneur d'Avesnes; died on the Third Crusade in the battle of Arsouf,
Palestine; fought under the leadership of Richard the Lion-Heart; son of
Nicholas d'Avesnes (RIN 1733) (d. 1169) and (m. bef 1150) Matilda
de la Roche (RIN 1734), daughter of Henry I, Lord de la Roche (this
line leads back to Louis IV, King of France. (Stuart, Line 50)

D'Avesnes, John I
(d. 1256)(RIN 581) Count of Holland. (Weis, 6th ed., Line 168)

Dammartin, Simon de
(d. 1239)(RIN 1031)
Count of Aumale; first husband of Marie, Countess of Ponthieu
(RIN 1032) (Weis, 6th ed., Line 144). Second son of Alberic II, Count
of Dammartin (d. 1200), and his wife Maud. (Weis, 6th ed., Line 109)

Edmund "Crouchback"
(d. 1296)(RIN 126) Earl of Lancaster and Leicester; son of Henry III (RIN 91); so named
because of the cross that was figured on the back of his clothes.
M. (1) Apr 1269 Aveline Fortibus (d. 1274), da. of William de Forz;
there was no issue of this marriage; he m. (2) Blanche (RIN 127),
widow of Henry, King of Navarre, da. of Robert, Count of Artois, and
granddaughter of Louis VIII (RIN 629) of France; in 1282 he captured
and beheaded Llewellyn ap Gruffyd; died at Bayonne while besieging
Bordeaux (*MC*, pg. 203; Weis, 6th ed., Line 45). Bur. near the altar in
Westminster Abbey. (*Westminster Abbey: Official Guide*, pg. 37)

Short Biographies

The Spear and the Spindle:
Ancestors of Sir Francis Bryan (d. 1550)
Bryan, Bourchier, Bohun, FitzAlan, and Others

```
                                                      King of England JOHN-152-(b.1166)-----
                                  K HENRY III-91-(b.1206)-------------
                                                      of Angouleme T ISABEL-151-(b.1186)----
    "Crouchback" EDMUND-126-(b.1244)-----
                                                      Raymund IV BERINGERUS-635-------------
                                  of Provence ELEANOR-92-(b.1217)------
                                                      of Savoy BEATRICE-636----------------
```

Edward I

(d. 1307)(RIN 89)   Edward "Longshanks." King of England 1272-1307. Crowned
19 August 1274; with Eleanor of Castile (RIN 90) had four sons and
nine daughters but only one son and five daughters survived infancy
(Canning, pg. 303; Weis, 6th ed., Line 1). For issue of Edward I and
Eleanor, see under Eleanor of Castile (RIN 90).

M. (2) 1298 Canterbury Cathedral Margaret of France (RIN 418)
(b. 1282, d. 1317), daughter of Philip III (RIN 579), King of France
(d. 1318). (Cotton) They were the parents of Edmund of Woodstock
(RIN 416) who was the father of Joan, "the Fair Maid of Kent"
(RIN 62), mother of Richard II.

In 1296 Edward took the Stone of Scone from Scotland (traditionally the
coronation seat of the Irish, then Scottish, kings; it now is contained
within the coronation chair Edward ordered built for it; the coronation
chair is kept in Westminster Abbey).

```
                                                      King of England JOHN-152-(b.1166)-----
                                  K HENRY III-91-(b.1206)-------------
                                                      of Angouleme T ISABEL-151-(b.1186)----
    K EDWARD I-89-(b.1239)--------------
                                                      Raymund IV BERINGERUS-635-------------
                                  of Provence ELEANOR-92-(b.1217)------
                                                      of Savoy BEATRICE-636----------------
```

Edward and Margaret had:
- Thomas of Brotherton, Earl of Norfolk (d. 1338)
- Edmund of Woodstock, 1st Earl of Kent (ex. 1330)
- Eleanor (d. 1311)

The Spear and the Spindle:
Ancestors of Sir Francis Bryan (d. 1550)
Bryan, Bourchier, Bohun, FitzAlan, and Others   Short Biographies

Edward I died at Burgh-by-Sands near Carlisle; bur. in the Confessor's Chapel in Westminster Abbey. (*Westminster Abbey: Official Guide*, pg. 37)

Edward II
(d. 1327)(RIN 1284)

King of England 1307-1327. Deposed and murdered. First Prince of Wales. M. Isabella of France (RIN 88) in the Church of Notre Dame in Boulogne. For his death at Berkeley Castle, Gloucester, see under Maurice Berkeley (RIN 1176). Bur. in Gloucester Cathedral.

For issue, see under Isabella of France.

Edward III
(d. 1377)(RIN 85)

King of England 1327-1377; began the Hundred Years War with France; founded Order of the Garter (Moncreiffe of that Ilk). Crowned 2 Feb 1327 (*KQB*). For issue by his first wife, see Philippa of Hainault (RIN 86). Died at Shene (Richmond) Palace, Surrey; bur. in Confessor's Chapel in Westminster Abbey (*Westminster Abbey: Official Guide*, pg. 37). (Stuart, Line 1)

```
                                                              K EDWARD I-89-(b.1239)----------------
                                    K EDWARD II-87-(b.1284)-------------
                                                              of Castile ELEANOR-90-(b.1244)--------
  K EDWARD III-85-(b.1312)-------------
                                                              K PHILIP IV-93-(b.1268)---------------
                                    of France ISABELLA-88-(b.1292)-------
                                                              de Navarre JEANNE-578-(b.1271)--------
```

Eleanor of Aquitaine
(d. 1204)(RIN 205)

Wife of Henry II (RIN 204), King of England; divorced in 1152 from her first husband, Louis VII (RIN 633), King of France.

By Louis, Eleanor had:
- Marie (RIN 1674) (b. 1145, d. 1198) m. Henry (RIN 1675), Count of Champagne
- Alix (b. 1150, d. 1197) m. Theobald V, Count of Blois (Meade, pg. x)

Eleanor and Henry had:
- William (d. infant; Cannon says at three years of age, pg. 141; buried at Reading in 1156, pg. 167)

Short Biographies

The Spear and the Spindle:
Ancestors of Sir Francis Bryan (d. 1550)
Bryan, Bourchier, Bohun, FitzAlan, and Others

- Henry (d. 1183); called "the young King" after his father had him crowned to secure the succession; however, his father survived him; Henry m. Margaret of France (d. 1198), daughter of Louis VII (RIN 633), King of France. Their child William died 1177 at birth. Margaret m. (2) Bela III (RIN 1593), King of Hungary.
- Matilda (d. 1189) m. Henry V the Lion, Duke of Saxony and Barvaria (d. 1195)
- Richard I the Lion-Heart, King of England 1189-1199, m. at Limassol Berengaria (d. abt 1231), daughter of Sancho VI, King of Navarre. There was no issue. Berengaria was crowned Queen, but she never set foot in England.
- Geoffrey, Duke of Brittany, m. Constance (d. 1201), daughter of Conan, Duke of Brittany; Geoffrey died 1185 in a jousting tournament; they had a son Arthur, Duke of Brittany (d. 1203), believed murdered by his uncle, John (RIN 152), King of England; had also a daughter, Eleanor (d. 1241). Constance m. (2) Ranulph, Earl of Chester; m. (3) Guy, Viscount of 1042 Thouars.
- Eleanor (RIN 1042) (d. 1214) m. Alfonso VIII (RIN 1041), King of Castile (d. 1214)
- Joanna (d. 1199) m. (1) William II, King of Sicily (d. 1189); m. (2) Raymond VIII, Count of Toulouse (d. 1222)
- John (RIN 152), King of England

(Usherwood)

Cannon (pg. 151) says Henry and Eleanor had nine children in thirteen years. Queen Eleanor was 45 when she gave birth to John, her last child (Josephine Ross, p. 31).

Eleanor was an energetic and remarkable (and often scandalous) woman. She travelled with her husband, Louis VII, to Palestine on the Second Crusade (1147-1149). She accompanied Berengaria to Cyprus to marry Richard the Lion-Heart (he was on his way to the Crusades in the Holy Land). One of her last journeys (when she was approaching 80 years of age) was to travel to Castile and fetch her granddaughter, Blanche (RIN 630), and take her to France to wed Louis (RIN 629), the heir to the French throne as Louis VIII.

A stained glass window in Poitiers Cathedral was given to the cathedral by Henry and Eleanor to commemorate their marriage there in 1152 (Cannon, pg. 90). Her ancestral home in Poitiers still stands and now serves as the Palace of Justice; some of the building additions were ordered by Eleanor herself. (Cotton; Meade, pgs. x, 18)

The Spear and the Spindle:
Ancestors of Sir Francis Bryan (d. 1550)
Bryan, Bourchier, Bohun, FitzAlan, and Others

Short Biographies

She died 1204, aged 82 years, and was buried in Fontevrault Abbey in Anjou with her husband, Henry II. Her favorite son, Richard the Lion-Heart was also buried there.

Eleanor of Castile
(d. 1290)(RIN 90)   Daughter of Ferdinand III (RIN 95), King of Castile and Leon; first wife (m. 1254) of Edward I (RIN 89) of England; she died 28 Nov 1290 at Harby, Nottinghamshire, while traveling with Edward, and her body was taken back to London; a cross was raised at each place her funeral cortege stopped for the night; three of the twelve Eleanor crosses remain (Labarge, pg. 41). Eleanor was buried in the Confessor's Chapel in Westminster Abbey, but her heart was buried in Blackfriars Church, London (*KQE*; *Westminster Abbey: Official Guide*, pg. 37). She was much loved by her subjects, and for more than 300 years, wax candles burned around her tomb in Westminster Abbey. She and Edward spent their wedding days at Leeds Castle.

Children include:
- Eleanor (d. 1298) m. (1) Alfonso, King of Aragon (d. 1291); m. (2) Henry, Count of Bar (d. 1302)
- Joan (d. young 1265)
- John, first born son (d. young 1272)
- Henry, second son, (d. 1274)
- Katherine (d. young 1271)
- Joanna, (b. at Acre, d. 1307) m. Apr 1290 Gilbert de Clare, Earl of Gloucester (d. 1295); m. (2) Ralph de Monthermer (d. 1325)
- Alphonso, third son (d. 1284)
- Margaret (d. 1318) m. John of Brabant (d. 1312)
- Berengaria (b. 1276, d. 1276/77)
- Mary became a nun (d. 1332)
- Isabella (d. young 1279)
- Alice
- Elizabeth (RIN 101) (d. 1316) m. (1) John Count of Holland, (d. 1299); m. (2) Humphrey de Bohun VIII (RIN 100)
- Edward II (RIN 87) (b. 1284, d. 1327), fourth son, succeeded his father; deposed by his queen; murdered
- Beatrice (d. young)
- Blanche (d. young)

There is a difference of opinion about the number of children—some references say 15, some 17, but only four sons are mentioned.

The Spear and the Spindle:
Ancestors of Sir Francis Bryan (d. 1550)
Bryan, Bourchier, Bohun, FitzAlan, and Others

Short Biographies

After the death of Eleanor, Edward I had erected stone crosses at the places where the funeral procession (4-14 Dec 1290) rested on the way from Nottinghamshire back to London: (1) Swine Green in Lincoln (a tomb in the Angel Choir in Lincoln Cathedral was constructed to contain the viscera of the queen); (2) St. Peter's Hill near Grantham; (3) Stamford; (4) Geddington, where the cross was raised over a spring; (5) Hardingstone near Northampton; (6) Stratford; (7) Woburn; (8) Dunstable; (9) St. Alban's; (10) Waltham; (11) Cheapside near London; (12) Charing (Cheringe). It is said that Cromwell's Roundheads destroyed all but three crosses. The present cross at Charing Cross is a reproduction. Strickland says there were thirteen crosses, but she does not list them (*Lives of the Queens of England*, "Eleanor of Castile").

Eleanor of England
(d.   )(RIN 1042)   Sister of King John of England (RIN 152) and daughter of Henry II (RIN 204), King of England, and his wife, Eleanor of Aquitaine (RIN 205). (*MC*, pg. 211)

Eleanor of Lancaster
(d. 1372)(RIN 105)   M. (1) bef Jun 1337 John de Beaumont (d. 1342); m. (2) 1344/45 Richard FitzAlan (RIN 104) (d. 1376), Earl of Arundel and Warenne; her great-grandfather was Henry III (RIN 91) (Weis, 6th ed., Line 17). For a listing of her children by second marriage, see under Richard FitzAlan (RIN 104). Eleanor was buried in the chapter-house of Lewes priory. (*D.N.B.*, "Richard II FitzAlan")

Eleanor of Provence
(d. 1291)(RIN 92)   Eleanor Berenger, daughter of Raymond, Count of Provence. Queen of Henry III (RIN 91) of England; crowned in Westminster Abbey 20 Jan 1236; she was buried in Convent Church, Amesbury, but her heart was buried in the Church of Friars Minors, London. (*KQE*)

```
                                                          King of Provence ALFONSO II-637-------
                                 Raymund IV BERINGERUS-635-----------
                                                          of Saban GERSENDA II-638-------------
 of Provence ELEANOR-92-(b.1217)------
                                                          of Savoy THOMAS I-641-(b.1177)--------
                                 of Savoy BEATRICE-636---------------
                                                          of Foucigny MARGUERITE-642-(b.1180)---
```

She and Henry had:
• Edward I (RIN 89)

The Spear and the Spindle:
Ancestors of Sir Francis Bryan (d. 1550)
Bryan, Bourchier, Bohun, FitzAlan, and Others

Short Biographies

- Margaret (d. 1275) m. Alexander III, King of Scotland
- Beatrice (d. 1275) m. John (d. 1305), Duke of Brittany, Earl of Richmond
- Edmund "Crouchback" (RIN 126), Earl of Lancaster (d. 1296); m. (1) Aveline, daughter of William de Forz, Count of Albemarle; m. (2) Blanche, daughter of Robert, count of Artois, son of Louis VIII (RIN 629), King of France, and widow of Henry, King of Navarre
- Richard (d. bef 1256)
- John (d. bef 1256)
- William (d. 1256)
- Kathering (d. 1257)
- Henry (d. young)

Ermensinde of Bar-sur-Seine
(d. 1211)(RIN 1742)

M. 1189 Theobald I (RIN 1741); she was the daughter of Gui (RIN 1745) (d. 1145), Count of Bar-sur-Seine, and Petronille of Chacenay (RIN 1746) (d. 1161). (Stuart, Lines 383, 384)

Eudoxia
(d.   )(RIN 1693)   Divorced in 1187 from William VIII (RIN 1694); she died a nun* (Weis, 6th ed., Line 105A). Stuart, Line 111, notes that her parentage is still under study. It is possible her parents were Alexies Komnenos (murdered 1183) and Marie Dukaina.

Ferdinand II, King of Leon
(d. 1188)(RIN 651)   Reigned 1157-1188 (*MC*, pg. 211). Son of Alphonso VII (RIN 1038) and Berenguela of Barcelona (RIN 1040).

Ferdinand III, King of Castile
(d. 1252)(RIN 95)   King of Castile 1217-1252; King of Leon 1230-1252. (*KQE*)

---

* It was not unusual for a woman of any marital status to retire to a convent, whether or not she "took the veil," and to remain there until her death.

Short Biographies

The Spear and the Spindle:
Ancestors of Sir Francis Bryan (d. 1550)
Bryan, Bourchier, Bohun, FitzAlan, and Others

```
                                                               King of Leon FERNANDO II-651----------
                                    K ALFONSO IX-649-(b.1166)------------
                                                               of Portugal URRACA-652---------------
           FERDINAND III-95-(b.1191)-----------
                                                               ALPHONSO VIII-1041------------------
                                    of Castile BERENGARIA-650-----------
                                                               of England ELEANOR-1042-(b.1162)------
```

Ferrers, William de
(d. 1254)(RIN 469)   7th Earl of Derby. Son of William Ferrieres (RIN 471) and Agnes Kevelioc of Chester (RIN 472). Bur. Merevale Abbey.

Ferrieres, William de
(d. 1247)(RIN 471)   6th Earl of Derby. One of the four Earls who bore the canopy at Richard I's second coronation; was present at the coronation of King John on 27 May 1199; present at the coronation of Henry III on 28 Oct. 1216; went on Crusade June 1218; was "long afflicted with the gout." (*CP*, Vol IV, Derby section). M. Agnes Kevelioc of Chester (RIN 472).

Fienes, Ingelram de
(d.   )(RIN 659)   Also Enguerrand de Fienes; Seigneur de Fienes. (Weis, 6th ed., Line 152)

Fienes, William de
(d. 1241)(RIN 660)   Also Guilleume de Fienes.

FitzAlan, Edmund
(d. 1326)(RIN 59)   Knighted 22 May 1306 by Edward I and at the same time married to Alice (RIN 60), sister of John, Earl of Warenne; 8th Earl of Arundel. He bore the royal robes at the coronation of Edward II.

Edmund was an enemy of Edward II's favorite, Piers Gaveston, and was one of the five earls who banded together against Gaveston and may have been present when Gaveston was captured and beheaded. However, he supported Edward II and agreed to marry his oldest son to the daughter of the younger Hugh Despenser. Even after the invasion by Edward II's Queen Isabella (RIN 88) and Mortimer (RIN 1182) (an invasion aimed at removing Edward II from the throne—it succeeded), Edmund continued to stand with the King. As a result, he was captured, led before the Queen at Hereford, and, on 17 Nov 1326, executed with little or no trial (*MC*, Chapter 249, pg. 2132; Weis, 6th ed., Line 28;

The Spear and the Spindle:
Ancestors of Sir Francis Bryan (d. 1550)
Bryan, Bourchier, Bohun, FitzAlan, and Others   Short Biographies

D.N.B., "Edmund FitzAlan"). For his issue, see Alice de Warenne (RIN 60).

FitzAlan, Joan
(d. 1404)(RIN 1653)

M. (1) Sir William de Brien; m. (2) abt 1401 Sir Wiliam de Echyngham (d. 20 Mar 1412/13). Weis, 6th ed., Line 59, says Joan d. 1 Sep 1404 and *Sureties*, Line 88, says Joan d. 1407. Joan was a descendant of Saher de Quency, a Magna Charta Surety, and of Hugh Capet, King of France. (Weis, 6th ed., Lines 59, 57, 53)

FitzAlan, Sir John
(d. 1379)(RIN 1654)

Marshal of England; 1st Lord Maltravers (Weis, 6th ed., Line 59). Perished at sea 1379 (*D.N.B.*, "FitzAlan, Richard II"). *Sureties* (Line 121-7) states that John died 15 Dec 1379.

```
                                                         Edmund FITZALAN-59-(b.1285)-----------
                              Richard II FITZALAN-104-(b.1313)-----
                                                         Alice de WARENNE-60-------------------
     Sir John FITZALAN-1654--------------
                                                         of Lancaster HENRY-108-(b.1281)-------
                              of Lancaster ELEANOR-105------------
                                                         Maud CHAWORTH-109--------------------
```

FitzAlan, John I
(d. 1240)(RIN 157) Of Clun and Oswestry, Salop.

FitzAlan, John II
(d. bef. 10 Nov 1267)(RIN 155)

Lord of Oswestry, Clun, and Arundel; though he is spoken of as Earl of Arundel, in all official documents he is referred to as simply John FitzAlan, and he referred to himself as simply Lord of Arundel; neither is his son, John (RIN 115), documented as Earl of Arundel; instructed his body to be buried at Haughmond, Shropshire. (*D.N.B.*, "FitzAlan, John II")

FitzAlan, Richard I
(d. 1302)(RIN 111) Earl of Arundel; he had two sons and two daughters by Alice/Alisona/Alasia; see under Alasia de Saluzzo (RIN 112). Richard was born "probably" 3 Feb 1267. In 1289 he was knighted by Edward I. Died 9 Mar 1302. (*D.N.B.*, "Richard I FitzAlan")

The Spear and the Spindle:
Ancestors of Sir Francis Bryan (d. 1550)
Bryan, Bourchier, Bohun, FitzAlan, and Others

Short Biographies

FitzAlan, Richard II
(d. 1375/76)(RIN 104)

"Copped Hat"; Justiciar of North Wales and Admiral of the West (*MC*, Chapter 249); m. (1) 9 Feb. 1320 to Isabel, daughter of Hugh Despenser and Alianore Clare (*MC*, pg. 955). Earl of Arundel and Warenne; m. (2) 5 Feb 1344/45 Eleanor Plantagenet (RIN 105) (Weis, 6th ed., Line 17). His marriage to Isabel Despenser, the daughter of the younger Hugh Despenser (a favorite of Edward II), was designed to cement the relationship between his father and the Despensers. However, in 1345 he repudiated Isabel (even though he had had a daughter by her), saying he had not agreed to the marriage. He received papal recognition of the nullity of the union and then married Eleanor (RIN 105), widow of Lord Beaumont and daughter of Henry of Lancaster (RIN 108).

Richard and Eleanor had three sons and four daughters:
- Richard III (RIN 30), his father's successor (Richard III's son Thomas died without issue)
- John (RIN 1654), marshal of England (he perished at sea 1379)
- Thomas, archbishop of Canterbury
- Joan (RIN 1616) m. Humphrey Bohun (RIN 1615), Earl of Hereford
- Alice (RIN 39) m. Thomas Holland (RIN 38), Earl of Kent
- Mary (died before her father)
- Eleanor (died before her father)

He was made Justice of North Wales for life (appointed 1334); appointed sheriff for life of Carnarvonshire; governor of Carnarvon Castle. In 1344 he was made lieutenant of Aquitaine.

Richard "Copped Hat" was extremely wealthy, frequently lending money to Edward III. Upon his death, much of his ready cash was found stored in bags in the high tower of Arundel. He instructed that he should be buried without pomp in Lewes priory.

He died 24 Jan 1376 and was buried in the chapter house of Lewes priory beside Eleanor. (*D.N.B.*, "Richard II FitzAlan")

FitzBernard, Ralph
(d.   )(RIN 870)   Of Kingstown, Kent.

The Spear and the Spindle:
Ancestors of Sir Francis Bryan (d. 1550)
Bryan, Bourchier, Bohun, FitzAlan, and Others   Short Biographies

FitzGeoffrey, John FitzPiers

(d. 1258)(RIN 175)   Sheriff of Yorkshire; Justice of Ireland (*MC*, Chapter 249); of Shere,
Farnbridge; Justiciar of Ireland 1245-1256; son of Geoffrey Fitz Piers,
Earl of Essex, and Aveline de Clare (Adams)

FitzGeoffrey, Maud FitzJohn

(d.   )(RIN 125)   Her marriage to William de Beauchamp was her second marriage (*MC*,
Chapter 249). M. (1) Gerard de Furnivalle of Sheffield, co. York,
d.s.p. 23 Nov. 1258; (2) bef. 1270 William de Beauchamp (RIN 123).
(Adams)

```
┌─────────────────────────────────────────────────────────────────────────────┐
│                                                        Geoffrey FITZPIERS-251----------------│
│                             John FitzPiers FITZGEOFFREY-175------                             │
│                                                        Aveline de CLARE-619-----------------  │
│  FitzJohn Maud FITZGEOFFREY-125-------                                                         │
│                                                        Hugh THE SURETY BIGOD-177------------   │
│                             Isabel BIGOD-176--------------------                               │
│                                                        Maud MARSHALL-178--------------------   │
└─────────────────────────────────────────────────────────────────────────────┘
```

FitzGeoffrey, Maud

(d. 1236)(RIN 248)   Maud Fitz Geoffrey de Mandeville; Countess of Essex. (Weis, 6th ed.,
Line 97)

FitzGerald, Maurice

(d. 1257)(RIN 1717)
Son of Gerald FitzMaurice (RIN 1719) and Eve de Bermingham
(RIN 1720). (Weis, 6th ed., Line 178)

FitzMaurice, Gerald

(d. 1203/04)(RIN 1719)
First Baron of Offaly; Weis (6th ed., Line 178) says that his wife, Eve
de Bermingham (RIN 1720) brought Offaly to her husband. First
husband of Eve de Bermingham.

FitzMaurice, Maurice

(d. 1286)(RIN 326)   Maurice FitzMaurice FitzGerald; Lord of Offaly in Ireland, Justiciar.
(Weis, 6th ed., Line 178)

FitzPiers, Geoffrey

(d. 1213)(RIN 251)   4th Earl of Essex. (Weis, 6th ed., Line 97)

Short Biographies

The Spear and the Spindle:
Ancestors of Sir Francis Bryan (d. 1550)
Bryan, Bourchier, Bohun, FitzAlan, and Others

Fitzroy, Richard
(d.   )(RIN 1713)   Natural son of John (RIN 152), King of England. (Weis, 6th ed., Line 26)

Florent III
(d. 1190)(RIN 1670)
B. abt 1138; d. on Crusade 1 Aug 1190, Antioch/Tyrus; Count of Holland, Earl of Ross. (Weis, 6th ed., Line 100; Stuart, Line 72)

Florent IV
(d. 1245)(RIN 1667)
Count of Holland. (Weis, 6th ed., Line 100)

Gersenda II
(d.   )(RIN 638)   Of Saban; Forcalquier.

Godfrey
(d. 1139)(RIN 1759)
B. abt 1067, d. 19 Aug 1139, bur. Florette; Count of Dagsburg; m. abt 1101 Ermesinde of Luxemburg (RIN 1760) (b. abt 1075, d. 24 Jun 1143). (Stuart, Lines 126, 3)

Godfrey III
(d. 1186)(RIN 1704)
B. 1142, Louvain, Brabant, France; d. 10 Aug 1190; bur. St. Peter's Church, Louvain;, Count of Louvain; Duke of Brabant and of Lower Lorraine; m. in 1155 Margaret von Limburg (RIN 1737) (Stuart, Line 68; Weis, 6th ed., Line 155). According to Weis Lines 155 and 148, this line goes back to Charlemagne the Great.

Gui
(d. 1145)(RIN 1745)
Count of Bar-sur-Seine. (Stuart, Line 383)

Guise, Adele de
(d.   )(RIN 1732)   B. abt 155; daughter of Bernard de Guise (RIN 1735) (living 1185) who m. bef 1150 Adelaide/Alix (RIN 1736). (Stuart, Line 34)

Helen of Galloway
(d.   )(RIN 80)   The daughter of Alan, Lord of Galloway, by his first wife, a daughter of Hugh de Lacy (d. 1243); also Helen MacDonel. (Weis, 6th ed., Line 38)

The Spear and the Spindle:
Ancestors of Sir Francis Bryan (d. 1550)
Bryan, Bourchier, Bohun, FitzAlan, and Others   Short Biographies

Henry
(d. 1181)(RIN 1675)
Count of Champagne. (Weis, 6th ed., Line 102)

Henry I
(d. 1182)(RIN 1764)
B. 1117; Count of Guelders; m. 1135 Agnes von Arnstein. (Stuart, Line 304)

Henry I
(d. 1235)(RIN 1574)
Duke of Brabant. (Weis, 6th ed., Line 155)

Henry II
(d. 1189)(RIN 204)   King of England 1154-1189. Eldest of three sons of Count Geoffrey V (RIN 204) of Anjou (Josephine Ross, pgs. 35, 41) and Matilda "the Empress" (RIN 207). Crowned 19 December 1154 (*MC*). M. Eleanor of Aquitaine (RIN 205). For issue, see under of Eleanor of Aquitaine.

To assure the peaceful transition of rule upon his death, Henry II had his eldest surviving son, Henry, crowned; the ceremony took place in 1170, and young Henry became known as "the young King."

The young King was married to Margaret of France, the daughter of Louis VII (RIN 633) by his second wife, Constance of Castile (Louis was Queen Eleanor's ex-husband); Henry was crowned 1170; Margaret and Henry were crowned together in a second ceremony in 1172 by the Archbishop of Rouen; however, young Henry died in 1183, his father outliving him. The young King was buried in Rouen Cathedral. (Cannon, pgs. 141, 148-149; *KQB*, pg. 54)

Henry II is most often remembered for his quarrel with Thomas Becket, his affair with Rosamonde, and the rebellion of his sons and wife (he imprisoned Eleanor for 12 to 15 years because she fomented strife between Henry and his sons). (Cannon, pg. 151)

Henry d. 6 Jul 1189 at Chinon Castle. He was buried at Fontevrault Abbey in Anjou. The tombs of Eleanor of Aquitaine and their son, Richard the Lion-Heart, are also there.

Short Biographies

The Spear and the Spindle:
Ancestors of Sir Francis Bryan (d. 1550)
Bryan, Bourchier, Bohun, FitzAlan, and Others

Henry II

(d. 1247/48)(RIN 1510)

Son of Henry I (RIN 1574), Duke of Brabant, and Maud of Alsace (RIN 1575).

Henry II

(d. 1167)(RIN 1753)

B. abt 1110; d. Aug 1167, Rome; Duke of Limburg; Count of Arlon. (Stuart, Line 71)

Henry III

(d. 1272)(RIN 91) King of England 1216-1272; extensively remodelled Westminster Abbey; in 1269 he had the bones of Edward the Confessor (in Westminster Abbey) placed in a new coffin, and Henry and his brother and son, Edward (Edward I), bore the coffin to its new location in the new shrine behind the altar of Westminster Abbey. Upon Henry's death 16 Nov 1272, his body was placed in the old coffin of Edward the Confessor and buried temporarily in front of the altar of Westminster Abbey. It was later moved to the tomb in the Confessor's Chapel of Westminster Abbey. Henry III was the first king since the Norman conquest to be buried in Westminster Abbey (Usherwood). Bur. in Confessor's Chapel of Westminster Abbey. (*Westminster Abbey: Official Guide*, pg. 37)

For issue, see under Eleanor of Provence (RIN 92).

```
                                                         K HENRY II-204-(b.1133)--------------
                          King of England JOHN-152-(b.1166)----
                                                         of Aquitaine ELEANOR-205-(b.1122)-----
K HENRY III-91-(b.1206)--------------
                                                         Aymer de TAILLEFER-622---------------
                          of Angouleme T ISABEL-151-(b.1186)---
                                                         Alix de (Courtenay) JOIGNY-623--------
```

Henry III of Luxembourg

(d. 1281)(RIN 1666)   Henry III "the Blond,"; Count of Luxemburg. (Stuart, Line 71)

Henry of Lancaster

(d. 1345)(RIN 108) Henry Plantagenet; Earl of Lancaster; a descendant of John (RIN 152), King of England (*MC*, Chapter 249). A grandson of Henry III (RIN 91), King of England (RIN 91). (Adams)

The Spear and the Spindle:
Ancestors of Sir Francis Bryan (d. 1550)
Bryan, Bourchier, Bohun, FitzAlan, and Others

Short Biographies

```
                                                              K HENRY III-91-(b.1206)--------------
                              "Crouchback" EDMUND-126-(b.1244)-----
                                                              of Provence ELEANOR-92-(b.1217)-------
   of Lancaster HENRY-108-(b.1281)------
                                                              ROBERT-129-(b.1216)--------------
                              of Artois BLANCHE-127---------------
                                                              of Brabant MATILDA-213---------------
```

Huntingdon, Ada de
(d. aft 1205)(RIN 1669)

B. abt 1146, Scotland; m. 1162 Florent III (RIN 1670), Count of Holland and Earl of Ros; her paternal grandfather was David I "the Saint" (RIN 283), King of Scotland. (Weis, 6th ed., Line 100; Stuart, Line 72)

Isabel de Angouleme
(d. 1246)(RIN 151) Isabella Taillefer; daughter of Aymer de Taillefer (RIN 622). Second wife of John (RIN 152), King of England; crowned 8 Oct 1200 in Westminster Abbey; m. (2) Hugh le Brun (RIN 150). At the time of her coronation, she was about twelve years old. (Cannon, pg. 140)

```
                                                              William IV de TAILLEFER-624----------
                              Aymer de TAILLEFER-622--------------
                                                              Emme de LIMOGES-625------------------
   of Angouleme T ISABEL-151-(b.1186)---
                                                              P PIERRE/PETER-1200-(b.1125)----------
                              Alix de (Courtenay) JOIGNY-623-------
                                                              ELIZABETH-1201----------------------
```

John and Isabella had:
- Henry III (RIN 91) (b. 1 Oct 1207)
- Richard (b. 6 Jan 1209, d. 1272), Earl of Cornwall, King of the Romans 1256, m. (1) Isabel (RIN 368) (d. 1240), daughter of William Marshal (RIN 179), Earl of Pembroke. She was widow of Gilbert de Clare (RIN 367), the Surety and Earl of Gloucester. Richard m. (2) Sanchia (d. 1261), daughter of Raymond Berengar (RIN 635), Count of Provence, and sister of Henry III's queen, Eleanor (RIN 92); m. (3) Beatrice, daughter of William de Fauquemont, Count of Montjoye
- Jane/Joan (d. 1238) m. Alexander, King of Scots

Short Biographies

The Spear and the Spindle:
Ancestors of Sir Francis Bryan (d. 1550)
Bryan, Bourchier, Bohun, FitzAlan, and Others

- Eleanor (RIN 1495) (d. 1275) m. (1) William Mareschal/Marshal the younger, Earl of Pembroke; m. (2) Simon Montfort (RIN 1494), Earl of Leicester
- Isabella m. Emperor Frederick II of Germany

Queen Isabel m. (2) Hugh le Brun (RIN 150), Count de la Marche. Their children included:
- Alice le Brun (RIN 120)
- Hugh XI le Brun (RIN 1387)

Isabel was buried with John's parents at Fontevrault Abbey, Anjou, where she died.

Isabella of France
(d.   )(RIN 88)

Also Isabelle; called the "She-Wolf" of France. M. Edward II (RIN 87), King of England; daughter of Philip IV (RIN 93), King of France; sister of Philip V, King of France and Navarre (d. 1322), and of Louis X, King of France and Navarre (d. 1316); crowned Queen of England 25 Feb 1308 in Westminster Abbey (*KQB*). Along with her lover, Roger de Mortimer (RIN 1182), she was responsible for deposing her husband (and probably for having him murdered) and putting her son, Edward III (RIN 85), on the throne. For fuller particulars, see under Maurice Berkeley (RIN 1176).

Children of Edward II and Isabella were:
- Edward III (RIN 85), King of England
- John, Earl of Cornwall (d. 1336 at age 20)
- Joan/Joanna (d. 1362) m. David II Bruce, King of Scotland
- Eleanor (d. 1355) m. Reynald, Duke/Count of Gueldres, (d. 1343) (Montague-Smith)

After his accession, Edward III sent his mother to live at Castle Rising, Norfolk, where she died at age 63. She was buried in the Grey Friars Church, London. Her lover, Roger Mortimer, was also buried there.

Isabella was sister of three French kings: Louis X, Philip V "the Long," and Charles IV "the Fair." Their father was Philip IV "the Fair," son of Philip III "the Bold," son of Louis IX "the Saint," son of Louis VIII "the Lion," son of Philip II Augustus, son of Louis VII "the Young," son of Louis VI "the Fat," son of Philip I, son of Henry I, son of Robert "the Pious," son of Hugh Capet, who was descended from Charlemagne the Great. (de Castries, Table "The Direct Capetians")

The Spear and the Spindle:
Ancestors of Sir Francis Bryan (d. 1550)
Bryan, Bourchier, Bohun, FitzAlan, and Others

Short Biographies

Isabella of Hainaut

(d. 1190)(RIN 632) First wife of Philip II "Augustus" (RIN 631); by him had one son and twin sons who died at birth. (*KQB*)

Jacques

(d.   )(RIN 658) Seigneur of Conde, Bailleul and Moriammez in Hainault. (Weis, 6th ed., Line 152)

James I

(d. 1276)(RIN 736) King of Aragon 1213-1276 (Weis, 6th ed., Line 105A). The Conqueror; m. (1) 1221 Eleanor (d. 1253), daughter of Alphonso VIII (marriage dissolved 1229); m. (2) Yolande/ Violante (RIN 1442); m. (3) Teresa Gil de Vedaura (d. 1276). (Previte-Orton)

Jeanne of Navarre

(d. 1304/05)(RIN 578)

Jeanne I, Queen of Navarre; wife of Philip IV "the Fair" (RIN 93), King of France, and mother of Isabella (RIN 88), the "She-Wolf," who married Edward II (RIN 87) of England. (*KQE*; Plaidy)

John

(d. 1216)(RIN 152) Son of Henry II (RIN 204), King of England, and his queen, Eleanor of Aquitaine (RIN 205). King of England 1199-1216; father of Henry III. John's marriage in 1189 to Hadwissa (also called Isabelle), daughter of William, Earl of Gloucester, was the first time that a legitimate son of the English ruling monarch had married an Englishwoman since before Cnut's conquest. The marriage ended in divorce in 1199; there was no issue. Hadwissa m. (2) Geoffrey de Mandeville; m. (3) Hubert de Burgh.

John m. (2) 1200 Isabella Taillefer (RIN 151) of Angouleme. For issue, see under Isabella of Angouleme.

John followed his brother, Richard the Lion-Heart, to the throne. In 1215 he was forced to concede to his barons and sign the Magna Charta; however, the disputes between John and the barons continued, and the future French King was invited to take over the throne of England. Prince Louis arrived and took London with little effort. John, fleeing, lost his treasure in the Wash River. He died 19 Oct 1216, perhaps from poisoning, in Newark Castle, Nottinghamshire. Bur. Worcester Cathedral.

Short Biographies

The Spear and the Spindle:
Ancestors of Sir Francis Bryan (d. 1550)
Bryan, Bourchier, Bohun, FitzAlan, and Others

Joigny, Alix de
(d.   )(RIN 623)   Alice de Courtenay (Weis, 6th ed., Line 117). B. abt 1160, d. abt
                    14 Sep 1205/1218. Daughter of Pierre/Peter (RIN 1200), Prince of
                    France, and Elizabeth (RIN 1201).

Keveliok, Hawise
(d. abt. 1242)(RIN 460)
                    Countess of Lincoln. (*MC*, Part IV)

Kuthan
(d.   )(RIN 1678)   Prince of Kumans. (Weis, 6th ed., Line 103)

Lacie, John de
(d. 1240)(RIN 356) Earl of Lincoln; Surety for the Magna Charta.

Lascaris I
(d. 1222)(RIN 1590)
                    Theodore Komnenos Lascaris I; also Theodore I; Emperor (Basilius) of
                    the East, 1204; b. 1173; d. abt Aug 1222; m. as her second husband in
                    1199 Anna Angelina (RIN 1765). Their daughter, Marie Laskarina
                    (RIN 1589) m. Bela IV (RIN 1588), King of Hungary. (Stuart, Line 74)

Limburg, Margaret von
(d. 1172)(RIN 1737)
                    B. abt 1139; m. bef 1155 Godfrey III (RIN 1704), Duke of Louvain.
                    (Stuart, Line 62)

Louis VII "the Young"
(d. 1180)(RIN 633) Louis Florus; King of France 1137-1180; crowned 25 October 1131 at
                    Rheims as successor to his father and again at Bourges 25 December
                    1137 after the death of his father; m. (1) 22 July 1137 at Bordeaux
                    Eleanor of Aquitaine (RIN 205), but this marriage was annulled on the
                    grounds of consanguinity in 1152 and Eleanor went on to marry Henry
                    Plantagenet (RIN 204), who would become Henry II of England.

                    By Eleanor, Louis had:
                    ● Marie (RIN 1674) (b. 1145, d. 1198) m. Henry I (RIN 1675)
                       (d. 1181), Count of Champagne
                    ● Alix (b. 1150, d. 1197) m. Theobald V, Count of Blois (d. 1191)
                    (Meade, pg. x)

                    Louis m. (2) 1154 at Orleans Constance of Castile; issue by Constance
                    included:

The Spear and the Spindle:
Ancestors of Sir Francis Bryan (d. 1550)
Bryan, Bourchier, Bohun, FitzAlan, and Others   Short Biographies

- Margaret (d. 1197) m. Henry "the Young King" (d. 1183), son of Eleanor of Aquitaine and Henry II; Margaret m. (2) Bela III, King of Hungary (RIN 1593) (d. 1196)
- Adelaide

Louis m. (3) 13 November 1160 Adele (RIN 634); by Adele, Louis had:
- Philip II "Augustus" (RIN 631), King of France
- Alice of France (RIN 1034), who was betrothed to Richard the Lion-Heart, son of Eleanor of Aquitaine and Henry II; Alice and Richard never married; she m. William II (RIN 1035), Count of Ponthieu
- Agnes m. (1) Alexis II Comnenus, Byzantine Emperor (d. 1183); m. (2) Andronicus I Comnenus (d. 1185), Byzantine Emperor; m. (3) Theodore Branas.

(*KQE*, pg. 188; Barber; Stuart, Lines 148, 243; Previte-Orton, pg. 462)

Louis was buried in the Abbey of Barbeaux, Melun.

Louis VIII "the Lion"
(d. 1226)(RIN 629) King of France 1223-1226; eldest son of Philip II (RIN 631) and Isabella of Hainaut (RIN 632); crowned 6 August 1223 at Rheims (*KQE*); died at Montpensier, Auvergne, France; bur. St. Denis.

Louis IX "the Saint"
(d. 1270)(RIN 225) "Louis Sanctus," King of France 1226-1270; crowned 29 November 1226 at Rheims; canonized in 1297 (*KQE*); bur. St. Denis. Canonized by Pope Boniface VIII. (*Enc. Brit.*)

Maltravers, John
(d. 1364)(RIN 1663)
Lord Maltravers/Maultravers; knighted 22 May 1306 (Weis, 6th ed., Line 59). For his part in the murder of Edward II, see under Maurice Berkeley (RIN 1176).

Margaret of Hainaut
(d. 1280)(RIN 594) Margaret of Hainaut; Margaret of Flanders. Countess of Hainaut and Flanders. (Weis, 6th ed., Line 168)

Margarite of Faucigny
(d. 1257)(RIN 642) Margaret of Geneva (Weis, 6th ed., Line 133). Daughter of William I of Geneva (RIN 1709).

The Spear and the Spindle:
Ancestors of Sir Francis Bryan (d. 1550)
Bryan, Bourchier, Bohun, FitzAlan, and Others

Short Biographies

Margarite of Lorraine
(d. 1194)(RIN 598) Heiress of Flanders; m. (1) abt 1160 Rudolph II, Count of Vermandois (d. 17 Jun 1167); m. (2) 1169 Baldwin V (RIN 597) (Weis, 6th ed., Line 165). Died 15 Nov 1194 (Stuart, Line 73).

Maria
(d.   )(RIN 1691) Daughter of William VIII of Montpellier (RIN 1694) and his wife, Eudoxia (RIN 1693). Bur. St. Peter's.

Marie, Countess
(d. 1250/51)(RIN 1032)

Countess of Ponthieu; m. (2) Mathieu de Montmorenci, Seigneur d'Attichy (d. 1250). (Weis, 6th ed., Line 144)

```
                                                            Count of Ponthieu JEAN I-1035---------
                                 WILLIAM III-1033-(b.1179)-----------
                                                            of St. Pol BEATRICE-1036-------------
        Countess MARIE-1032-----------------
                                                            K LOUIS VII-633-(b.1119)-------------
                                 of France ALICE-1034----------------
                                                            of Castile CONSTANCE-972-(b.1134)-----
```

Marie, Princess
(d. 1323)(RIN 1584)

Of Hungary.

Marie, Princess
(d. 180)(RIN 1576) Mary of Blois; b. abt 1135, Blois, France; d. 25 Jul 1180/82; daughter of Stephen (RIN 1578), King of England, and Matilda of Boulogne (RIN 1579). (Stuart, Lines 299, 205)

Marie of Champagne
(d. 1204)(RIN 596) Daughter of Henry I, Count of Champagne (b. abt 1126), d. 17 Mar 1181, Troyes) who m. 1164 Marie of France (RIN 1674) (b. 1145, d. 11 Mar 1198). Marie of Champagne was granddaughter of Louis VII (RIN 633), King of France. (Weis, 6th ed., Line 102; Stuart, Lines 137, 134)

The Spear and the Spindle:
Ancestors of Sir Francis Bryan (d. 1550)
Bryan, Bourchier, Bohun, FitzAlan, and Others   Short Biographies

Marie of France
(d. 1198)(RIN 1674)

B. 1145, d. 11 Mar 1198; daughter of Louis VII (RIN 633) and his first wife Eleanor of Aquitaine (RIN 205). In 1164 she married Henry, Count of Champagne. (Weis, 6th ed., Line 102; Stuart, Line 134)

Marshall, Eve
(d.   )(RIN 256)

Sister and coheir of Richard (Marshal), Earl of Pembroke, Marshal of England. (*CP*, Vol. IX, Mortimer)

```
                                                                John MARESCHALL-182------------------
                                    William MARSHALL-179-(b.1153)--------
                                                                Sibyl DEVEREUX-183-------------------
        Eve MARSHALL-256--------------------
                                                                Richard de CLARE-187-----------------
                                    Isabel de CLARE-180-(b.1173)---------
                                                                Eve/Eva MACMURROUGH-188--------------
```

Marshall, Isabella
(d. 1240)(RIN 368)

Sister of William Marshall, Earl of Pembroke and a Surety for the Magna Charta (he died issueless) (*MC*, pgs. 31, 920). Daughter of William Marshall (RIN 179), Earl of Pembroke Marshal of England. Isabella m. (1) Gilbert de Clare (RIN 367), Earl of Gloucester (d. 1230); m. (2) Richard, Earl of Cornwall (d. 1272), son of John (RIN 152), King of England, and Isabella of Angouleme (RIN 151).

Marshall, Maud
(d. 1248)(RIN 178)

A sister of the Magna Charta Surety, William Marshall (who died issueless) (*MC*, pg. 31 and Chapter 249); daughter of William Marshall (RIN 179), Earl of Pembroke. (*MC*, Part IV)

Marshall, William
(d. 1219)(RIN 179)

"The Protector"; Earl Marshal of England and Earl of Pembroke and Striguil. Son of John Marshal (RIN 182) (d. 1165) (Duby, pg. 66) and his second wife Sibyl of Salisbury (RIN 183) (Duby, p. 62). His paternal grandfather was Gilbert (d. abt 1130), marshal of the court for Henry I (Duby, pgs. 58, 59, 60). William served five kings of England—Henry II, Henry the young King, Richard I, John, and Henry III. William Marshall was described by historians as the most perfect and loyal knight, soldier, and statesman; his loyalty to his king never wavered, yet he never compromised his honor.

Short Biographies

The Spear and the Spindle:
Ancestors of Sir Francis Bryan (d. 1550)
Bryan, Bourchier, Bohun, FitzAlan, and Others

He was in charge of Henry II's eldest son and heir, Henry, who was crowned King while his father was still alive (and therefore was called "the young King"). William was with the young King when he became ill and died at Martel 11 Jun 1183. As requested by him, William bore the young King's cross to the Holy Land, where his exploits were most successful.

William was present at the death of Henry II and escorted the body for burial to Fontevrault.

He married Isabella (RIN 180), daughter of Richard de Clare (RIN 187), Earl of Pembroke and Striguil. For issue see under Isabel de Clare (RIN 180).

He carried the gold sceptre at Richard I's coronation 3 Sep 1189 (William's elder brother, John, carried the spurs). After Richard's death, William declared for Richard's youngest brother, John, as heir to the throne (others favored John's nephew, Arthur). He was present at Runnymede as one of the royal representatives and a counsellor of Magna Charta. He was present at Gloucester 28 Oct 1216 when King John's son was crowned Henry III. William was regent during early life of Henry III until the King assumed full power in January 1227.

John Earley, squire to Marshall, in 1220s wrote a biography of William Marshall.

Before his death on 14 May 1219 (Duby, pg. 20), William assumed the habit of a Templar, and, at his own request, was buried in the Temple Church in London (*D.N.B.*, "Marshal"). His effigy can still be seen.

Matilda de Bar of Lingy
(d. 1275)(RIN 1738)
> Also Margaret. (Stuart, Line 36)

Matilda of Brabant
(d. 1288)(RIN 213) Sister of Henry III, Duke of Brabant (d. 1291). (Weis, 6th ed., Line 155)

The Spear and the Spindle:
Ancestors of Sir Francis Bryan (d. 1550)
Bryan, Bourchier, Bohun, FitzAlan, and Others

Short Biographies

```
                                                      Duke of Brabant HENRY I-1574----------
                              HENRY II-1510-----------------------
                                                      of Alsace MAUD-1575------------------
  of Brabant MATILDA-213--------------
                                                      K PHILIP II-1511-(b.1177)------------
                              of Germany MARY-1509----------------
                                                      IRENE ANGELA-1512--------------------
```

Matilda/Maud "the Empress"

(d. 1167)(RIN 207) "The Empress"; "Queen Matilda"; daughter of Henry I (RIN 210), King of England, and his first wife, Matilda of Scotland (RIN 211) (d. 1118), daughter of Malcolm III (RIN 278), King of Scotland. (Moncreiffe of that Ilk)

At age twelve, she m. (1) 1114 Mainz Cathedral Henry V, Emperor of Germany (d. 23 May 1125), who was thirty years older than she; there was no issue. She was much loved by the German people.

Her brother, William, drowned in the wreck of the White Ship in 1120. After the death of the Emperor, Henry called his daughter back to England. For political reasons, he married her in 1128 to Geoffrey V (RIN 206), Count of Anjou and Maine (marriage dates differ in sources; the given is taken from Weis who took it from the *CP*). Geoffrey Plantagenet was ten years younger than Matilda, and the marriage was a stormy one: Matilda had been an Empress and resented being married to a mere boy and count.

Henry I m. (2) Adelicia (d. 1151), daughter of Geoffrey, Duke of lower Lorraine, but there was no issue. Henry made his barons swear to accept Matilda as his heir to the throne. However, after Henry's death in 1135, the barons split their support between Matilda and her cousin, Stephen (son of William the Conqueror's daughter, Adela), and a long and devastating war followed. Stephen's nineteen-year reign was described as a time "when God and his angels slept."

Matilda was never crowned. Her German arrogance and monetary demands turned the English people against her, and, at one time, they chased her from London.

Matilda was sixty-four when she died. (Murray)

Short Biographies

The Spear and the Spindle:
Ancestors of Sir Francis Bryan (d. 1550)
Bryan, Bourchier, Bohun, FitzAlan, and Others

Matilda and Geoffrey had:
- Henry II (RIN 204), King of England
- Geoffrey, Count of Nantes (d. 1158)
- William, Count of Poitou (d. 1164) (Cotton)

See also Hameline Plantagenet (RIN 191).

Matthieu of Alsace
(d. 1174)(RIN 1577)

B. abt 1137, d. 25 Jul 1173; bur. Josse; m. 1160 Princess Marie/Mary of Blois (RIN 1576), daughter of Stephen (RIN 1578), King of England. Count of Bologne (Stuart, Line 205). His mother was Sibyl, a sister of Geoffrey Plantagenet (*MC*, pg. 603).

Maud of Alsace
(d. 1210)(RIN 1575)

Maud/Matilda of Flanders; b. abt 1160/65, d. 1211, Louvain; daughter of Matthieu of Alsace (RIN 1577) and Princess Marie (RIN 1576). First wife (m. 1179) of Henry I (RIN 1574), Duke of Brabant (d. 5 Oct 1235). (Weis, 6th ed., Line 155; Stuart, Line 205)

Maud of Ponthies
(d. aft Oct 1200)(RIN 663)

Also Matilda. Daughter of Renaud II (RIN 1775), Count of Clermont (d. abt 1162) and Clemence of Bar-le-Duc (RIN 1774) (d. aft 20 Jan 1183).

Maudit/Mauduit William
(d. 1220)(RIN 454) Earl of Warwick.

Mortimer, Ralph de
(d. 1246)(RIN 705) Brother of Hugh de Mortimer (Hugh m. bef. 1210 Eleanor (Annor), daughter of William de Braose/Briouze and Maude de St. Valery. (*CP*, Vol. IX, Mortimer)

Mortimer, Roger de
(d. bef. 10 Oct 1282)(RIN 226)

Knighted by King Henry III (RIN 91) at Winchester at Whitsuntide 1253; fought on the March against his cousin Llewelyn ap Griffith, leader of the Welsh chieftains; on 19 May 1260, he was appointed constable of Hereford Castle; Mortimer commanded the rearguard at Evesham on 4 Aug 1265; after Montfort's death his head was sent to Mortimer's wife at Wigmore; the Mortimers seem to be into heads, as

The Spear and the Spindle:
Ancestors of Sir Francis Bryan (d. 1550)
Bryan, Bourchier, Bohun, FitzAlan, and Others   Short Biographies

in 1282 his son Edmund (RIN 511) took Llewelyn's head to the King at Rhuddland. The Complete Peerage says that Edmund Mortimer was not there when Llewelyn was killed but identified the body after death. From Rhuddland, the head of Llewelyn was delivered to London where it was set on a spike on the Tower and crowned with ivy (*CP*, Vol. IX, Mortimer). 6th Baron Mortimer of Wigmore. Son of Ralph de Mortimer (RIN 705) and Gladys "Dark Eyes" Dhu (RIN 704). Bur. Wigmore.

Otto I
(d. 1207)(RIN 1673)

Count of Guelders and Zutphen. (Weis, 6th ed., Line 100)

Pedro II
(d. 1213)(RIN 1692)

King of Aragon, Count of Barcelona and Gevandur; died while fighting for the Albigensians in Battle of Muret 13 Sep 1213; he was the third husband of Marie (RIN 1691). (Weis, 6th ed., Line 105A)

Peter
(d.)(RIN 1200)   Prince of France, Lord of Courtenay and Auxerre; the fifth son of King Louis VI of France (*MC*, pg. 187). Crusader in 1147; present in England in 1178. (Weis, 6th ed., Line 117)

Petronille of Chacenay
(d. 1161)(RIN 1746)

Also Elizabeth of Chacenay; living 1135-1161. (Stuart, Line 384)

Philip II
(d. 1208)(RIN 1511)

King of Germany. B. 1177/1181, d. 21 Jun 1208, Bambert, Germany. Murdered by Otto of Wittlesbach; Duke of Swabia; Margrave of Tuscany, Emperor of Germany 1198. (Weis, 6th ed., Line 45)

Philip II "Augustus"
(d. 1223)(RIN 631)   King of France 1180-1223; crowned 1 November 1179 at Rheims; m. (1) Isabelle of Hainaut (RIN 632); m. (2) 14 August/5 November 1193 at Amiens Ingeborg, daughter of Valdemar I, King of Denmark, and Sophie of Poltsk; m. (3) 1 June 1196/1200 Agnes, daughter of Berthold VI, Duke of Meran, and Agnes of Wettin-Rochlitz. (*KQE*)

Philip III "the Bold"
(d. 1285)(RIN 579)   King of France 1270-1285; crowned at Rheims 15 August 1271; m. (1) Isabelle (RIN 580) and by her had four sons; m. (2) Marie

Short Biographies

The Spear and the Spindle:
Ancestors of Sir Francis Bryan (d. 1550)
Bryan, Bourchier, Bohun, FitzAlan, and Others

(RIN 1382) and by her had one son and two daughters; Philip III was buried at St. Denis, his entrails being buried at Narbonne Cathedral (*KQE*). Also called Philip le Hardi and Philip Audax. Bur. St. Denis.

Philip IV "the Fair"
(d. 1314)(RIN 93)   King of France 1285-1314; crowned at Rheims on 6 January 1286; by Jeanne I, Queen of Navarre (RIN 578), had four sons and three daughters (*KQE*). Bur. St. Denis. (Weis, 6th ed., Line 45)

Philippa of Hainault
(d. 1369)(RIN 86)   Queen of Edward III; daughter of William, Count of Hainault and Holland; crowned March 1330 in Westminster Abbey. (*KQB*)

```
                                                        Count of Hainaut JOHN II-575----------
                                WILLIAM III-94----------------------
                                                        of Luxembourg PHILIPPA-576-----------
of Hainault PHILIPPA-86-(b.1311)-----
                                                        CHARLES-1583-(b.1270)----------------
                                of Valois JEANE-577----------------
                                                        Princess MARGARET-1582---------------
```

Children of Edward and Philippa were:
- Edward, Prince of Wales; called "the Black Prince" either for the color of his armor or for his mood/temper; b. 15 June 1330 Woodstock, d. 8 June 1376 Trinity Sunday; m. Joan, "the Fair Maid of Kent" (RIN 62) (d. 1385); she was daughter of Edmund, Earl of Kent, son of Edward I (RIN 89), and widow of Thomas Holland, Earl of Kent; the Black Prince and Joan had Richard II of England (Richard had no issue)
- Lionel, Duke of Clarence (d. 1368) m. (1) Elizabeth de Burgh (d. 1363), daughter of William de Burgh
- John of Gaunt (RIN 34), Duke of Lancaster (d. 1399), m. (1) Blanche of Lancaster, (2) Constance of Castile, and (3) Catherine de Roet Swynford (RIN 35)
- Edmund of Langley, Duke of York (d. 1402), m. (1) Isabel, daughter of Pedro III, King of Castile; m. (2) Joan Holland, daughter of Thomas Holland, Earl of Kent
- Thomas (RIN 1611), Duke of Gloucester; called Thomas of Woodstock; murdered 1397; m. Eleanor Bohun (RIN 1612), daughter of Humphrey Bohun (RIN 1615), Earl of Hereford, Essex and Northampton (Cotton; Montague-Smith)
- William (d. 1337)

The Spear and the Spindle:
Ancestors of Sir Francis Bryan (d. 1550)
Bryan, Bourchier, Bohun, FitzAlan, and Others

Short Biographies

- William (d. 1348)
- Thomas (d. young)
- Isabel (d. 1382) m. Ingelram de Coucy, Earl of Bedford (d. 1397)
- Joanna (d. 1348)
- Blanche (d. young)
- Mary (d. 1362) m. John de Montfort, Duke of Brittany (d. 1399)
- Margaret (d. 1361) m. John Hastings, Earl of Pembroke (d. 1375)

(Montague-Smith).

Philippa d. 1369 at Windsor. Bur. in Confessor's Chapel, Westminster Abbey (*Westminster Abbey: Official Guide*, pg. 37). (Stuart, Line 50)

Plantagenet, Anne
(d. 1438)(RIN 1613)

Daughter of Thomas of Woodstock (RIN 1611), youngest son of Edward III (RIN 85) and his wife Alianore/Eleanor de Bohun (RIN 1612). Anne m. (1) 1392 Thomas, 3rd Earl of Stafford (d. 1392); m. (2) 1398 Edmund, 5th Earl of Stafford (d. 21 Jul 1403, Battle of Shrewsbury), brother of Thomas, 3rd Earl.

By her second marriage she had Humphrey Stafford, 1st Duke of Buckingham.

She m. (3) 20 Nov 1404/05 William Bourchier (RIN 1614), Count of Eu.

Her children by William were:
- Henry (d. 4 Apr 1483), Earl of Essex, Viscount Bourchier
- Thomas, Archbishop of Canterbury (d. 1486), who was involved with the "Princes in the Tower"
- William, Lord FitzWarin (from whom descended the earls of Bath)
- John (RIN 1617), Lord Berners, ancestor of Sir Francis Bryan (RIN 1626)
- Anne (d. 16 Oct 1438) (Clive, pg. 22)

Plantagenet, Geoffrey V
(d. 1151)(RIN 206) Count of Anjou and Maine; Duke of Normandy (Moncreiffe of that Ilk). Second husband of Matilda, "the Empress." For issue, see under Matilda (RIN 207). See also Hameline Plantagenet (RIN 191).

Plantagenet, Hameline
(d. 1202)(RIN 191) M. Isabel Warren (RIN 192) (*MC*). According to Weis (6th ed., Line 123), Hameline was the son of Geoffrey V (RIN 206), Count of

Short Biographies

The Spear and the Spindle:
Ancestors of Sir Francis Bryan (d. 1550)
Bryan, Bourchier, Bohun, FitzAlan, and Others

Anjou, by an unknown mistress; Weis's source for this is the Complete Peerage. He m. as her second husband Isabella (RIN 192), daughter of William de Warenne, Earl of Surrey.

Quency, Roger de
(d. 1264)(RIN 58)   Earl of Winchester. M. (2) Maud, Countess of Pembroke, daughter of Humphrey de Bohun, Earl of Hereford and Essex; m. (3) Alianore (d. 26 Oct. 1274), seventh daughter of William de Ferrers (RIN 469) and Sibyl la Mareschale (RIN 470) (*MC*, pg. 114). 2nd Earl of Winchester; Constable of Ireland (Weis, 6th ed., Line 38). Son of Saher de Quency (RIN 128) (d. 1219), a Surety for the Magna Charta.

Quincy, Saire de
(d. 1219)(RIN 128)   Earl of Winchester; Magna Charta Surety (*MC*, Part IV); governor of the castle of Ruil in Normandy; created Earl of Winchester in 1207; was one of the Barons who invited the Dauphin of France, Prince Louis, to take the throne of England in place of King John; was at the siege of Damietta 1219 in the Holy Land; died on his way to Jerusalem (*MC*, pg. 112).

Quincey, Hawise de
(d.   )(RIN 134)   Daughter of the Magna Charta Baron, Saire de Quincey (RIN 128). (*MC*, Chapter 249)

Quincey, Margaret de
(d. bef 12 Mar 1281)(RIN 611)
Margaret of Groby.

Raoul I de Coucy
(d. 1191)(RIN 1747)
B. abt 1135, d. Nov 1191, Acre (on the Third Crusade), bur. Foisny; m. as his first wife bef 1164 Agnes of Hainault (RIN 1748), (b. abt 1142, d. 1168/1173), daughter of Baldwin IV (RIN 599), Count of Hainault, and Alice de Nemur (RIN 600). (Stuart, Line 37)

Renaud II
(d. 1170)(RIN 1743)
B. abt 1115, d. 25 Jul 1170; m. 1155 Agnes of Blois (RIN 1744) (b. abt 1138, d. 7 Aug 1207). (Stuart, Line 36)

Ridelisford, Emmeline de
(d. 1276)(RIN 216)   Daughter of Lord Walter de Ridelisford of Bray (RIN 217) (d. bef 12 Dec 1244) and Annora (RIN 1721). (Weis, 6th ed., Line 33)

The Spear and the Spindle:
Ancestors of Sir Francis Bryan (d. 1550)
Bryan, Bourchier, Bohun, FitzAlan, and Others

Short Biographies

Robert I
(d. 1188)(RIN 1395)

B. abt 1123; d. 11 Oct 1188; bur. St. Ived, Braine; Count of Dreux, Perche, and Braine; his father was Louis VI "the Fat" (RIN 761), King of France. According to Stuart (Line 124), Robert I was married three times: (1) 1139/1141 Agnes de Garlande (b. abt 1122, d. 1143); (2) 1144 Hawise (b. abt 1118, d. 1152), widow of Rotrou II, Count of Perche, and daughter of Walter, Count of Salisbury, and Sibylle de Chaworth; and (3) 1152 Agnes de Baudemont (Vaudemont) (RIN 1396) (d. bef 1218), who was mother of Robert II (RIN 1393), Count of Dreux. Weis, 6th ed., Line 135, lists the third wife and her father as Vaudemont.

Robert, Count of Artois
(d.   )(RIN 129)

Son of Louis VIII, King of France 1223-1226, and brother of St. Louis IX, King of France 1226-1270 (*KQE*) and Charles of Anjou (RIN 1676), King of Naples. Count of Artois. (Weis, 6th ed., Line 113)

```
                                                              K PHILIP II-631-(b.1165)-------------
                               K LOUIS VIII-629-(b.1187)-----------
                                                              of Hainault ISABELLA-632-(b.1170)-----
         ROBERT-129-(b.1216)-----------------
                                                              ALPHONSO VIII-1041--------------------
                               of Castile BLANCHE-630-(b.1188)------
                                                              of England ELEANOR-1042-(b.1162)------
```

Saffenburg, Matilda von
(d. 1145)(RIN 1754)

Daughter of Adalbert von Saffenberg; d. 2 Jan 1145. (Stuart, Line 71)

Saluzzo, Alasia de
(d. 1292)(RIN 112)

Wife of Richard III FitzAlan (RIN 111), Earl of Arundel; they had two sons and two daughters:
- Edmund (RIN 59)
- John
- Maud m. Philip, Lord Burnell
- Margaret m. William Botiler of Wem (*D.N.B.*, "Richard I FitzAlan")

Bur. Todingham Priory.

Short Biographies

The Spear and the Spindle:
Ancestors of Sir Francis Bryan (d. 1550)
Bryan, Bourchier, Bohun, FitzAlan, and Others

Sancho III, King of Castile
(d. 1158)(RIN 1043)

Sancho III the Desired; reigned 1157-1158; m. Blanca/Blanche of Navarre (RIN 735), daughter of Garcia IV of Navarre. (*KQE*, pg. 42; *MC*; Previte-Orton, Table 22)

Saunford, Alice
(d.   )(RIN 122)   Also Sanford.

Simon I
(d. 1181)(RIN 1756)

Count of Saarbrucken; d. 23 Jun 1181/1182, m. Matilda von Sponheim (RIN 1757) (b. abt 1127). (Stuart, Lines 23, 365)

Stephen V
(d. 1272)(RIN 1586)

King of Hungary 1270-1272. (Weis, 6th ed., Line 103)

Tallefer, Aymer de
(d.   )(RIN 622)   Also Taillefer; also Aymer de Valence. Count of Angouleme; the father of Isabella (RIN 151), wife of John (RIN 152), King of England (*MC*, pg. 187). Son of William IV Taillefer (RIN 624) and Marguerite de Turenne (RIN 1199). (Stuart, Lines 156, 87; Weis, 6th ed., Line 153)

Thibault I
(d. 1201)(RIN 1567)

Count of Brie; son of Henry I, Count of Champagne (RIN 1675) (d. 17 Mar 1181, Troyes) and Marie of France (RIN 1674) (d. 11 Mar 1198), daughter of Louis VIII (RIN 633), King of France, and his first wife, Eleanor of Aquitaine (RIN 205). (Stuart, Line 81)

Thomas I of Savoy
(d. 1177)(RIN 641)   Count of Savoy (Weis, 6th ed., Line 133). Son of Humbert III (RIN 643) (d. 1188), Count of Savoy, and Beatrix of Vienne (RIN 644).

Thomas of Woodstock
(d. 1397)(RIN 1611)

Fifth and youngest son of Edward III by his wife Philippa of Hainault; progenitor of the Stafford (Buckingham) families; created Duke of Gloucester by Richard II in 1385, and in 1397 he was murdered, supposedly on the King's orders (St. Aubyn, 1983). *D.N.B.* ("Thomas of Woodstock") says Thomas was the seventh and youngest son, so he

The Spear and the Spindle:
Ancestors of Sir Francis Bryan (d. 1550)
Bryan, Bourchier, Bohun, FitzAlan, and Others

Short Biographies

was probably considered the fifth surviving son of Edward III. Knighted by his father 23 Apr 1377 at Windsor. Styled Earl of Essex in right of his wife, Eleanor Bohun (RIN 1612). His chief home was Pleshy Castle, Essex.

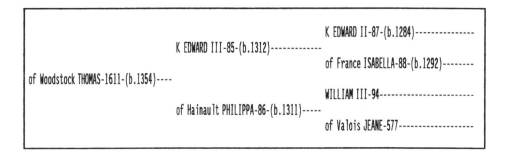

```
                                                              K EDWARD II-87-(b.1284)--------------
                                K EDWARD III-85-(b.1312)------------
                                                              of France ISABELLA-88-(b.1292)--------
of Woodstock THOMAS-1611-(b.1354)----
                                                              WILLIAM III-94----------------------
                                of Hainault PHILIPPA-86-(b.1311)-----
                                                              of Valois JEANE-577-----------------
```

His wife was the elder daughter of Humphrey Bohun IX (RIN 1615), and Thomas had custody of the vast inheritance of the younger sister, Mary. However, Mary was the ward of John of Gaunt, Thomas's brother. Relations were poor between John and Thomas and were not helped when John put his son, Henry (soon to be Henry IV), up for the order of the Garter, effectively blocking Thomas from that honor (Thomas was created a Knight of the Garter April 1380). John also denied Thomas Mary's inheritance by marrying the younger sister to his own son and dashing any hopes on Thomas's part that Mary would choose the life of a nun and leave her inheritance to Thomas and Eleanor.

Thomas, uncle to Richard II, carried the sceptre at Richard's coronation in 1377. He was one of those who objected to the poor rule of the king and as good as threatened to remove Richard from his throne. To make a long story short, King Richard, having had enough of Thomas, arrested him at Pleshy Castle and sent him to Calais to be imprisoned under the eye of the Earl of Nottingham. A few weeks later, early in September, it was announced in Calais and England that Thomas had died 25/26 August. However, Sir William Rickhill, justice of the common pleas, was sent by King's orders to Calais on 7 September to interview Thomas, which he did on 8 September, surprised to find the prisoner alive. He was puzzled, too, to see that his orders were dated 17 August. However, he questioned Thomas as instructed and received a written confession from him. When Rickhill returned the next day to see Thomas again, he was denied admittance. When Parliament met on 17 September and called for the appearance of Thomas, it was announced that he was dead, and the written confession was read in Parliament, those portions being omitted which were contrary to what

Short Biographies

The Spear and the Spindle:
Ancestors of Sir Francis Bryan (d. 1550)
Bryan, Bourchier, Bohun, FitzAlan, and Others

Richard wanted to hear. We must assume the confession was undated; therefore, those not "in the know" would assume that Thomas had died the 25/26 August as rumored and that the confession had been written before then.

Why the timing of the confession was important is only conjecture, but perhaps Richard did not want Thomas present in Parliament yet did not want him to die at the last moment before Parliament met, which would look suspicious. As it is, Thomas's death goes down as murder and it rests on Richard II's head.

After Richard was deposed, Halle, a servant of the Earl of Nottingham, Thomas's jailer, swore that King Richard ordered Thomas's death and that Thomas was smothered with a feather bed by one of Richard's servants. Both Halle and the murdering servant were executed (*D.N.B.*, "Thomas of Woodstock") (St. Aubyn, 1983). Thomas was buried beside his mother and father in the Confessor's Chapel of Westminster Abbey. His wife, Eleanor, was buried nearby in the Chapel of St. Edmund in Westminster Abbey. (*Westminster Abbey: Official Guide*)

For issue, see Eleanor Bohun (RIN 1612).

Tommaso I, Marquis
(d.)(RIN 117)   Tommaso of Saluzzo. Marquis of Saluzzo in Piedmont. (Weis, 6th ed., Line 28)

Tylney, Elizabeth
(d. 1497)(RIN 1620)

M. (1) Sir Humphrey Bourchier (RIN 1619); m. (2) 30 Apr 1472 Sir Thomas Howard (b. 1443, d. 21 May 1524), Earl of Surrey, Duke of Norfolk; by her second marriage, she was mother of Elizabeth Howard, the wife of Sir Thomas Boleyn and mother of Queen Anne Boleyn; Elizabeth Tylney d. 4 Apr 1497. (Ives 1986; Weis, 6th ed., Line 22; *Sureties*, Line 63)

Tylney, Frederick
(d.)(RIN 1621)   Of Boston Co., Lincs. (*Sureties*, Line 18)

Urraca of Portugal
(d. 1176/78)(RIN 652)

Daughter of Alphonso I (RIN 1044), King of Portugal, and Maud of Savoy (RIN 1045).

The Spear and the Spindle:
Ancestors of Sir Francis Bryan (d. 1550)
Bryan, Bourchier, Bohun, FitzAlan, and Others

Short Biographies

Vaudemont, Agnes de
(d. bef 1218)(RIN 1396)

Third wife of Robert I (RIN 1395), Count of Dreux; widow of Milon II of Bar-sur-Seine and daughter of Guy de Vaudemont, Count of Braine, and wife Alix/Adelaide. (Stuart, Line 124, says Baudemont. Weis, 6th ed., Line 135, says Vaudemont)

Vere, Hugh de
(d. bef. 23 Dec 1263)(RIN 133)

4th Earl of Oxford (*MC*'). Son of Robert de Vere (RIN 137), the Magna Charta Surety, and Isabel de Bolebec (RIN 138).

Vere, Robert de
(d. 1296)(RIN 121) 5th Earl of Oxford and sixth great Chamberlain. (*MC*, Chapter 249, pg. 2132)

```
┌─────────────────────────────────────────────────────────────────────────────┐
│                                                    Robert de THE SURETY VERE-137---------│
│                         Hugh de VERE-133-(b.1210)-----------                   │
│                                                    Isabel de BOLEBEC-138----------------│
│  Robert de VERE-121-(b.1240)----------                                         │
│                                                    Saher IV de T QUENCY-128-(b.1154)-----│
│                         Hawise de QUINCEY-134---------------                    │
│                                                    Margaret BELLOMONT-130---------------│
└─────────────────────────────────────────────────────────────────────────────┘
```

Vere, Robert de
(d. 1221)(RIN 137) Surety for the Magna Charta; 3rd Earl of Oxford; hereditary Lord Great Chamberlain of England; eighth in descent from Hugh Capet. D. bef 25 Oct 1221. (*MC*, Chapters 249, 119). Baptized 1164 (Weis, 6th ed., Line 60)

Warenne, Alice de
(d. bef. 23 May 1338)(RIN 60)

Wife of Edmund FitzAlan (RIN 59), Earl of Arundel, and daughter of William de Warren (RIN 113). Sister of John, Earl of Warenne.

Children of Edmund and Alice were:
- Richard II FitzAlan (RIN 104), eldest son, who received the title and estates upon the death of his father
- Edmund, who, for a while, seemed to be in the ecclesiastical profession
- Aleyne m. Roger L'Estrange/Strange
- Alice m. John Bohun, Earl of Hereford

The Spear and the Spindle:
Ancestors of Sir Francis Bryan (d. 1550)
Bryan, Bourchier, Bohun, FitzAlan, and Others

Short Biographies

- Jane "said to have married" Lord Lisle. The *D.N.B.* here suggests comparing other sources. (*D.N.B.*, "Edmund FitaAlan")

Warren, John de
(d. 1302)(RIN 119) 7th Earl of Warren and Surrey, son of William Plantagenet de Warren (RIN 181) and Maud Marshall (RIN 178).

```
                                                              Hameline PLANTAGENET-191-------------
                                 William de Plantagenet WARREN-181----
                                                              Isabel Countess WARREN-192-----------
         John de WARREN-119------------------
                                                              William MARSHALL-179-(b.1153)--------
                                 Maud MARSHALL-178-------------------
                                                              Isabel de CLARE-180-(b.1173)---------
```

Warren, William de
(d. 1240)(RIN 181) William Plantagenet de Warren; son of Hameline Plantagenet (RIN 191) and Isabel, Countess Warren (RIN 192).

Warren, William de
(d. 1285/1286)(RIN 113)
7th Earl of Surrey; killed in a tournament at Croyton (*MC*, Chapter 249, pg. 2132; Weis, 6th ed., Line 60)

William I
(d. 1223/24)(RIN 1671)
Count of Holland and Zealand. (Weis, 6th ed., Line 100)

William I
(d. 1195)(RIN 1709)
Count of Geneva 1178-1195; Weis says "perhaps (though doubtful)" that his wife was Beatrix de Faucigny, daughter of Aimon I of Faucigny and of Clementia. (Weis, 6th ed., Line 133)

William III
(d. 1221)(RIN 1033)
Count of Ponthieu; son of Jean I (RIN 1035), Count of Ponthieu, and Beatrice of St. Pol (RIN 1036).

William III
(d. 1337)(RIN 94) Count of Hainault and Holland. (Weis, 6th ed., Line 168; Stuart, Line 50)

The Spear and the Spindle:
Ancestors of Sir Francis Bryan (d. 1550)
Bryan, Bourchier, Bohun, FitzAlan, and Others   Short Biographies

William VIII
(d. 1218)(RIN 1694)

Seigneur de Montpellier; divorced in 1187 from Eudoxia (RIN 1693). (Weis, 6th ed., Line 105A)

William X
(d. 1137)(RIN 212)   Father of Eleanor of Aquitaine (RIN 205); named "the Toulousain" after the city of his birth; had a huge appetite and quarrelsome nature; d. on Good Friday, 9 Apr 1137, on pilgrimage to Compostela; he left Eleanor his fief and willed both Eleanor and his domains to Louis, King of France (RIN 633); he was buried in the cathedral of Compostela at the foot of the high altar. (Meade, pg. 32)

Wittelsbach, Richardis von
(d. 1231)(RIN 972)   D. 7 Dec 1231; m. bef 1188 Otto I (RIN 1673). (Stuart, Line 307)

Yolande de Courtenay
(d. 1233)(RIN 1724)

Second wife of Andreas II/Andrew II (RIN 1591), King of Hungary; mother of Yolande/Violante (RIN 1442). Her father was Peter II de Courtenay (RIN 1028), Count of Courtenay, and Emperor of the East 1217 (b. abt 1155, d. aft Jun 1219, m. 1 Jul 1193 Yolande of Flanders (RIN 1027), Countess of Namur). (Stuart, Line 79)

Yolande of Hungary
(d. 1255)(RIN 1442)

Also Violente; second wife of James I, King of Aragon (RIN 763). (*KQE*; Previte-Orton)

Zouche, Sir Alan la
(d. 1269)(RIN 81)   4th Baron la Zouche; descended from the Earls of Brittany (*MC*, pg. 758). Baron Zouche of Ashby la Zouche, co. Leicester; he was Constable of the Tower of London. (Weis, 6th ed., Line 38)

Zouche, Sir Roger la
(d. 1238)(RIN 107)   Son of Alan la Zouche (RIN 259) (d. 1190).

Zouche, Eudo la
(d. 1279)(RIN 1180)

Of Haryngworth; young brother of Sir Alan La Zouche (RIN 81). (Weis, 6th ed., Line 38)

The Spear and the Spindle:
Ancestors of Sir Francis Bryan (d. 1550)
Bryan, Bourchier, Bohun, FitzAlan, and Others

Collaterals

The following people are not at this time on this family tree of Sir Francis Bryan but are related and interesting. They are included here for reference.

Bohun, Mary de
(d. 1394)

Sister of Eleanor de Bohun (RIN 1612). She married Henry of Bolingbroke (b. 1367 Bolingbroke, Lincolnshire), the son of John of Gaunt [q.v.].

They had issue:
- Henry V (b. Sep 1387); Henry of Monmouth
- Thomas, Duke of Clarence (d. 1421), m. Margaret Holland, daughter of Thomas Holland, Earl of Kent
- John, Duke of Bedford (d. 1435), m. (1) Anne (d. 1432), daughter of John the Fearless, Duke of Burgundy; m. (2) Jacquetta (d. 1472), daughter of the Count of St. Pol (she m. (2) Richard Woodville, 1st Earl Rivers, and had issue, Elizabeth, who m. Edward IV)
- Humphrey, Duke of Gloucester (d. 1447); m. (1) Jacqueline of Bavaria (d. 1436), Duchess of Hainault, Countess of Holland; they were divorced 1426; Humphrey m. (2) Eleanor, daughter of Lord Cobham
- Blanche m. Louis, Duke of Bavaria
- Philippa m. Eric VII, King of Denmark

(Previte-Orton, Table 23; *KQE*)

Mary died in childbirth Jun 1394. Henry IV later remarried; he had no issue by his second wife, Joan (d. 1437), daughter of Charles II, King of Navarre.

Bourchier, Henry
(d. 1458)

Second son of Henry Bourchier (d. 4 Apr 1483), Viscount Bourchier, Earl of Essex, and Isabel, daughter of the Earl of Cambridge by Anne Mortimer. He was the grandson of William Bourchier (RIN 1614); married Elizabeth Scales; Elizabeth later married Anthony, Queen Elizabeth Woodville's brother. (Clive, *This Son of York*, pg. 115)

Bourchier, Humphrey
(d. 1471)

Note that this Humphrey is *not* Humphrey Bourchier (RIN 1619) in the table of this manuscript. This Humphrey is Lord Cromwell, the third son of Henry Bourchier, Viscount Bourchier, Earl of Essex (d. 4 Apr 1483), by Isabel, the daughter of Richard, Earl of Cambridge, and sister of Edward IV's father. Henry Bourchier was brother of John Bourchier

The Spear and the Spindle:
Ancestors of Sir Francis Bryan (d. 1550)
Bryan, Bourchier, Bohun, FitzAlan, and Others   Collaterals

(RIN 1617), 1st Lord Berners, who was father of Sir Humphrey
Bourchier (RIN 1619). Adding to the confusion is that both Humphreys
died Easter, 14 Apr 1471, at the Battle of Barnet. See footnotes,
pg. 171, in Clive's *This Sun of York*.

Bourchier, John
(d. 1532/33)
2nd Lord Berners; son of Humphrey Bourchier (RIN 1619) and
Elizabeth Tylney (RIN 1620); brother of Margaret "Lady Bryan"
Bourchier (RIN 1624); uncle of Sir Francis Bryan (RIN 1626).

Shown favor by Henry VIII; Bourchier went as chamberlain to Henry's
sister, Princess Mary, on the occasion of her marriage to Louis XII of
France. Bourchier and his wife were present at the Field of Cloth of
Gold in 1520, where Henry VIII met with the French king, Francis I.

John became deputy of Calais in 1520.

He m. Catherine Howard, daughter of the Duke of Norfolk. Their
daughter Jane/Joan m. Edmund Knyvet of Ashwellthorp, Norfolk.
Bourchier also had illegitimate sons, Humphrey, James, and George.

He is known as the translator of Froissart's *Chronicles* and other works.

He died 16 Mar 1532/33. He was buried in the parish church of Calais.
(See *D.N.B.*, "John Bourchier")

Bourchier, John
Fourth son of Henry Bourchier (d. 4 Apr 1483), Viscount Bourchier,
Earl of Essex; brother of Humphrey, Lord Cromwell (d. 14 Apr 1471);
John Bourchier married (2) Elizabeth Ferrers, widow of Edward Grey,
Lord Ferrers of Groby. (Clive, *This Sun of York*, pg. 100)

Bourchier, John
John Bourchier, Earl of Bath, Count of Eu, was the son and heir of
John, the first Earl of Bath; the latter John was the son and heir of Fulk
Bourchier (also spelled Bourghchier), Lord Fitzwarin; Fulk was the son
and heir of William Bourchier, Lord Fitzwarin, the third son of William
Bourchier (RIN 1614) (d. 28 May 1420) and Anne Plantagenet
(RIN 1613). (*CP*, Eu section)

Bourchier, Thomas
(b. abt 1404, d. 1486)
Son of William Bourchier (RIN 1614), Count of Eu, and Anne
Plantagenet (RIN 1613), daughter of Thomas of Woodstock (RIN 1611)

Collaterals

The Spear and the Spindle:
Ancestors of Sir Francis Bryan (d. 1550)
Bryan, Bourchier, Bohun, FitzAlan, and Others

by Eleanor Bohun (RIN 1612); appointed Archbishop of Canterbury in 1454; made a Cardinal in 1467/1473; as Archbishop he crowned Edward IV 28 Jun 1461, Richard III 6 Jul 1483, and Henry VII 30 Oct 1485 and officiated at the marriage of Henry VII and Elizabeth of York 18 Jan 1486.

After the death of Edward IV in 1483, his queen, Elizabeth Woodville, fearing the protectorate of Edward IV's brother, Richard, took sanctuary in Westminster with her children. Richard, uncle of the two boys, already had in his protection/custody in the Tower Edward IV's eldest son and heir, Edward. Richard wanted the younger son of Edward IV, ten-year-old Richard, the 5th Duke of York, to leave sanctuary and join his brother in the Tower. Archbishop Bourchier, on 16 Jun arrived at Westminster Sanctuary with Gloucester, Lord Howard, and his son, Thomas. They persuaded, coerced, or forced the queen to give up her son.

Historians have wondered about the role of the Archbishop in this matter. Clive (pg. 284) says that the Archbishop could have been stupid in the matter or senile (he was about eighty years old if his given birth date is correct) or he could have been acting out of cowardice. Pollard has suggested that perhaps the Archbishop chose to go along in this matter in the hopes of avoiding a desecration of sanctuary by Richard's soldiers should they enter and forcibly take the child from his mother. At any rate, the prince was removed to the Tower where he joined his brother, the uncrowned Edward V. Three weeks later, the coronation ceremony took place as planned—except that when the ceremony was over, the new king of England was the uncle, Richard III—not Edward V.

The young boys were seen several times that summer playing in the yards of the Tower, until they were seen less and less often. They eventually disappeared. Tradition is that they were smothered in their sleep and their bodies buried under one of the staircases of the Tower. Almost two hundred years later, in 1674, while repairs were being made to a staircase, the bones of two children were discovered. Eventually, the bones were enclosed in an urn and placed in Westminster Abbey.

In Appendix I of his book, *Richard the Third*, Kendall presents the available evidence of the princes' deaths. The man who supposedly orchestrated the murder of Edward V and his brother was James Tyrell, a surname, interestingly enough, also found in the facts of the accidental death or assassination of William II, King of England—Walter Tirel.

The Spear and the Spindle:
Ancestors of Sir Francis Bryan (d. 1550)
Bryan, Bourchier, Bohun, FitzAlan, and Others   Collaterals

See also *The Plantagenet Encyclopedia*, "Thomas Bourchier"; *This Sun of York* by Mary Clive; *Richard III* by Pollard; *The Year of the Three Kings* by Giles St. Aubyn.

Bourchier, William
(d. aft. 12 Feb 1482/83)

Eldest son of Henry Bourchier, Viscount Bourchier, Earl of Essex, and his wife Isabel, daughter of Richard, Earl of Cambridge; m. bef 15 Aug 1467 Anne Woodville [q.v.] (d. 30 Jul 1489). Anne m. (2) as his first wife George (Grey), Earl of Kent (d. 21 Dec 1503).

Warkworth's Chronicle erroneously states that William Bourchier died at the Battle of Barnet in 1471. See *CP*, Essex section.

William Bourchier and Anne Woodville had a son, Henry Bourchier, Earl of Essex, Viscount Bourchier, Lord Bourchier, Count of Eu in Normandy, who was 11 years old or more in 1483. Henry (d. 13 Mar 1539/40) married abt 1498 Mary Say. They had a daughter, Anne, who was Henry's heir. Anne married in 1526/27 William Parr and became Baroness Bourchier. Parr was made Earl of Essex.

William Bourchier's father, Henry Bourchier (d. 4 Apr 1483), Viscount Bourchier, Earl of Essex, was brother of John Bourchier (RIN 1617), 1st Lord Berners.

Bryan, Elizabeth

Sister of Sir Francis Bryan (RIN 1626); she m. Sir Nicholas Carewe [q.v.], Kt. (ex. 1539). (Ives, genealogical table, pg. xvii)

Bryan, Margaret
(d. by 1521)

Sister of Sir Francis Bryan (RIN 1626); she m. Henry Guildford [q.v.], Kt. (d. 1532). (Ives, genealogical table, pg. xvii)

Carew, Sir Nicholas
(d. 1539)

Knight; Master of the Horse for Henry VIII; married Elizabeth Bryan, sister of Sir Francis Bryan (RIN 1626) (Ives, genealogical table). Carew was executed in 1539 for supporting the Princess Mary's restoration to the succession to the throne. (Henry VIII, after marrying Anne Boleyn, had declared Mary—his only child by Queen Katherine of Aragon—illegitimate and denied her right to succeed.) The thrust of the accusation of treason came from Lord Cromwell and was instrumental in manipulating Henry to see Carew's actions as a double loyalty, which Henry would not tolerate. He sentenced to death Carew and others who

Collaterals

The Spear and the Spindle:
Ancestors of Sir Francis Bryan (d. 1550)
Bryan, Bourchier, Bohun, FitzAlan, and Others

supported Mary. Eventually, Mary did become queen and is remembered as "Bloody Mary.") A picture of Nicholas Carew can be found in David Starkey's *The Reign of Henry VIII: Personalities and Politics*.

FitzAlan, Richard III
(d. 1397/98)

Son of Richard II FitzAlan (RIN 105) and Eleanor of Lancaster (RIN 105); brother of Sir John FitzAlan (RIN 1654) and Joan FitzAlan (RIN 1616). Knight of the Garter; Earl of Arundel and Surrey.

He was one of the five lords appellant who, dissatisfied with King Richard II's rule, advocated the capture and deposition of the King. Even though the King issued a royal pardon to the five, he personally never forgave FitzAlan; eventually, FitzAlan was declared a traitor. The traitor's death* was commuted to beheading, and FitzAlan died on Tower Hill. He was buried in the church of the Augustinian friars.

FitzAlan m. (1) Elizabeth de Bohun (RIN 31) (d. 1385), daughter of William de Bohun (RIN 98), Earl of Northampton, Earl of Hereford, and had issue. He m. (2) Philippa, daughter of the Earl of March and widow of John Hastings, Earl of Pembroke.

He was a religious man and generous to the church; he was of the brotherhood of the abbey of Tichfield. The common people admired him and after his death looked upon him as a saint; pilgrimages were made to his tomb. King Richard II saw this as a threat to his hold on the crown, so he had all traces of the tomb removed. However, after the death of the King, the pilgrimages resumed. (*D.N.B.*, "Richard III FitzAlan")

Guildford, Henry
(d. 1532)

B. 1489; Knight; Controller of the Household and Master of the Revels for Henry VIII; married Margaret Bryan, sister of Sir Francis Bryan (RIN 1626) (Ives, genealogical table). Master of the Horse; Controller of the Royal Household; Knight of the Garter (Williams, pg. 118). See

---

* The traitor's death was the most severe punishment meted out. It involved hanging the culprit, taking him down while he was still alive, cutting his intestines out (often to be burnt before his eyes), and quartering his body for dispersal to the four parts of the kingdom as a warning to others contemplating treason. Persons of the nobility could be condemned to a traitor's death, but out of respect for the noble blood the sentence could be lessened to death by beheading.

The Spear and the Spindle:
Ancestors of Sir Francis Bryan (d. 1550)
Bryan, Bourchier, Bohun, FitzAlan, and Others   Collaterals

Neville Williams' *Henry VIII and His Court*, pg. 118, for a painting of Henry Guildford. A Holbein sketch of Henry Guildford can be found in David Starkey's *The Reign of Henry VIII: Personalities and Politics*.

John of Gaunt
(d. 1399)(RIN 34)   Duke of Lancaster; son of Edward III (RIN 85), King of England, and Queen Philippa (RIN 86); brother of Thomas of Woodstock (RIN 1611).

John carried on the business government for his nephew, Richard II, until the King was old enough to take control of his country. Some historians have stated that John wanted to be king (and this could be true; he certainly would have made a better king than Richard II, who was eventually deposed), but all indications are that John respected Richard's position and served him well. John had hoped when married to his second wife Constance, to be king of Castile. Though he never became king of any country, a number of his children and grandchildren eventually had thrones of their own.

John m. (1) Blanche, daughter of Henry, Duke of Lancaster, and had:
● Henry IV, King of England; called Henry of Bolingbroke; m. Mary de Bohun [q.v.] They became parents of Henry of Monmouth (Henry V) who had Henry VI from whom descended the House of Lancaster.
● Philippa (d. 19 Jul 1415) m. John I, King of Portugal
● Elizabeth

John m. (2) Constance, daughter of Pedro/Peter III, King of Castile, and had:
● Katherine m. Henry III, King of Castile, from whom descended the Kings of Castile and Aragon

John m. (3) early in 1396 Katherine, daughter of Sir Payne de Roet and widow of Sir Hugh Swynford; they had:
● John Beaufort, Earl of Somerset (d. 1410), from whom descended Henry VII, King of England, and the House of Tudor and the Kings of Scotland
● Henry Beaufort (d. 1448), Cardinal, Bishop of Winchester, Lord Chancelor
● Thomas Beaufort, Duke of Exeter (d. 1426)

The Spear and the Spindle:
Ancestors of Sir Francis Bryan (d. 1550)
Bryan, Bourchier, Bohun, FitzAlan, and Others

Collaterals

● Joan m. (1) Sir Robert Ferrers; m. (2) Ralph Neville, 1st Earl of Westmoreland. From this second marriage descended Edward IV, Richard III, and the House of York.
(Hutchinson, pg. 13)

The story of Katherine and John of Gaunt is a romantic one (see *Katherine* by Anya Seton). Katherine was governess to John of Gaunt's children. She had her four children by John before they were married. After the death of John's second wife, John and Katherine were married. John, as Regent of England, was probably the most powerful man in England and certainly one of the wealthiest. His marriage with a mere governess was looked upon with much disapproval of the court and much envy and resentfulness from the ladies of the court.

In 1397, her children were made legitimate by Richard II but were barred from succession to the throne. John and Katherine became great-grandparents of Edward IV and Richard III.

Katherine died in 1403; she was buried by the High Altar in Lincoln Cathedral. Her daughter, Joan, was also buried there. (Montague-Smith; Barton)

Katherine's sister, Philippa de Roet, m. the poet Geoffrey Chaucer.

Mowbray, Eleanor
(d. 1481)

Da. of William Bourchier (RIN 1614) and Lady Anne Plantagenet (RIN 1613), and sister of John, Lord Berners (RIN 1617). M. John Mowbray, 3rd Duke of Norfolk (d. 1461), and had John, 4th Duke of Norfolk (d. 1476), through whom she became the grandmother of Anne Mowbray (b. 10 Dec 1472, d. 19 Nov 1481 Greenwich, bur. Westminster Abbey). Anne Mowbray m. 15 Jan 1478 at age 5 Richard, Duke of York (then age 4), second son of Edward IV, King of England, and his queen Elizabeth Woodville. The young Duke of York and his older brother, Edward V, were the two princes in The Tower who disappeared in 1483 and were believed to have been murdered by their uncle, Richard III, King of England (see **Bourchier, Thomas** in this section). (*D.N.B.*, "Thomas Bourchier (1401?-1486)"; Clive, *This Son of York*, pgs. 242-244; Virgoe, pg. 62)

Montfort, Simon V de
(d. 1265)(RIN 1494)

B. Normandy 1208?; fourth son of Simon IV de Montfort; Earl of Leicester 1231-1265; Governor of Gascony; was grand seneschal at the

The Spear and the Spindle:
Ancestors of Sir Francis Bryan (d. 1550)
Bryan, Bourchier, Bohun, FitzAlan, and Others   Collaterals

coronation of Henry III's (RIN 91) queen, Eleanor of Provence
(RIN 92).

M. 1238 Eleanor (RIN 1495), daughter of King John (RIN 152) of
England and sister of Henry III.

Montfort was among those who drew up the Provisions of Oxford,
designed to curb the royal power and appointed to oversee the
government. He joined a group of rebel barons and captured Henry III
at the Battle of Lewes. Became ruler in fact of England but suffered
devastating defeat at the Battle of Evesham Aug 1265 by Henry III's
son, Prince Edward (Edward I) (RIN 89). Simon died in battle and his
body was mutilated. He was buried at Evesham Abbey. (*Plantagenet
Encyclopedia*, pg. 138)

Richard the Lion-Heart
(d. 1199)

Son of Henry II (RIN 204) of England and Eleanor of Aquitaine
(RIN 205) and brother of John (RIN 152), King of England. Richard
was King of England 1189-1199. He spent approximately six months of
his 10-year reign in England. Fought in the Crusades. He married
12 May 1191 in Cyprus Berengaria of Navarre. There was no issue.

Berengaria was crowned Queen after the wedding ceremony, but she
never visited England.

Richard died 6 Apr 1199 in Chalus, Limousin, France, from a festering
arrow wound and was buried at Fontevrault Abbey, Anjou. Berengaria
died about 1230.

Woodville, Anne
(d. 30 Jul 1489)

Wife (m. bef 15 Aug 1467) of William Bourchier [q.v.] (d. aft 12 Feb
1482/3) and sister of Edward IV's queen, Elizabeth Woodville. Anne
was the third daughter of Richard Wydville/Woodville (RIN 9), Earl
Rivers, and his wife Jacquetta (RIN 50), daughter of Pierre of
Luxembourg (RIN 321), Count of St. Pol and Conversano. William
Bourchier's father was Henry Bourchier, Viscount Bourchier, Earl of
Essex, son of William Bourchier (RIN 1614) and Anne Plantagenet
(RIN 1613).

Anne m. (2) as his first wife George (Grey), Earl of Kent (d. 21 Dec
1503).

Collaterals

The Spear and the Spindle:
Ancestors of Sir Francis Bryan (d. 1550)
Bryan, Bourchier, Bohun, FitzAlan, and Others

By William Bourchier, Anne Woodville was mother of Henry Bourchier (b. abt 1472, d. 13 Mar 1539/40), Viscount Bourchier, Earl of Essex, Lord Bourchier, Count of Eu; he married (abt 1498) Mary Say and had a daughter and heir general, Anne, who in 1526/27, m. William Parr. She became Baroness Bourchier, and Parr was created Earl of Essex. See *CP*, Essex section.

The Spear and the Spindle:
Ancestors of Sir Francis Bryan (d. 1550)
Bryan, Bourchier, Bohun, FitzAlan, and Others

Collaterals

The Spear and the Spindle:
Ancestors of Sir Francis Bryan (d. 1550)
Bryan, Bourchier, Bohun, FitzAlan, and Others

Appendix A

Sir Francis Bryan Calls Anne Boleyn "Cousin"

At a time when family connections could be political statements, it was not uncommon for people to ride the royal favoritism shown to their kin. Sir Francis Bryan (RIN 1626) has been quoted as referring to Anne Boleyn as his "cousin" (see *D.N.B.*, "Sir Francis Bryan"). With much intermarrying among the king's court, there were innumerable instances of close and distant kinships. However, it is in the nature of a genealogist to delve into any hinted kinship (blood, step, or in-law). One such relationship is suggested here: in this case, the connection between Sir Francis Bryan and Queen Anne Boleyn.

Elizabeth Tilney/Tylney (RIN 1620), da. of Sir Frederick Tilney/Tylney (RIN 1621), m. Humphrey Bourchier (d. 14 Apr 1471, Battle of Barnet) (RIN 1619). They were the parents of Margaret Bourchier (RIN 1624). Margaret Bourchier m. Sir Thomas Bryan (RIN 1625) and had issue including Sir Francis Bryan (RIN 1626).

As widow of Humphrey Bourchier, Elizabeth Tilney Bourchier married (30 Apr 1472) as his first wife Sir Thomas Howard (b. 1443) (d. 21 May 1524), Earl of Surrey, Duke of Norfolk. They were the parents of Elizabeth Howard (d. 3 Apr 1537). Elizabeth Howard m. (by 1506) Sir Thomas Boleyn (b. abt 1477, d. 12 Mar 1538/39), Earl of Wiltshire, Earl of Ormond, and had issue including Queen Anne Boleyn and Mary Boleyn (mistress of Henry VIII and wife of William Cary).

Thus, Anne's maternal grandmother, Elizabeth Tilney Bourchier was the maternal grandmother of Sir Francis Bryan, and Sir Francis' mother and Anne's mother were half-sisters. This relationship may be one of the reasons Sir Francis referred to Anne as his "cousin."

A more distant relationship is also advanced here. Katherine Howard was the daughter of John Howard, Duke of Norfolk, slain and attainted 1485 (*CP*, Norfolk table), and Margaret (Wyfold) Norreys. This John Howard was father of the above-mentioned Thomas Howard (d. 1524).

Katherine married Sir John Bourchier, second Baron Berners (d. 19 Mar 1532), the brother of Sir Francis Bryan's mother. Thus Katherine Howard, too, became a cousin. She was also the half-sister of said Thomas Howard, Duke of Norfolk (d. 1524), father of Anne Boleyn's mother (Weis, 6th ed., Line 16).

The Spear and the Spindle:
Ancestors of Sir Francis Bryan (d. 1550)
Bryan, Bourchier, Bohun, FitzAlan, and Others

Appendix A

Hackett (pg. 153) says that the Howard women had married into the Bryan, Wyatt, Boleyn, and Ap Rice families, so there were many such "cousins."

At the time Anne Boleyn was in the ascendancy at court, i.e., wooed by Henry VIII, Henry showed favor to her by showing favor to her relatives. Not that Sir Francis needed Anne's help; he had been held in great affection by Henry long before Anne's appearance at court. It was surely because of this affection that Sir Francis escaped the danger surrounding Anne Boleyn when Henry decided to rid himself of her and marry Jane Seymour. Sir Francis was an intelligent man and knew Henry well enough to sense what was coming. It was an act of self-preservation when Sir Francis deserted his "cousin" and left her to her fate on the scaffold. Because of this seeming callousness, Cromwell called Bryan "the Vicar of Hell" (*D.N.B.*, "Sir Francis Bryan (d. 1550)") (also seen as "the one-eyed Vicar of Hell").

For fuller particulars, see Weis, 6th ed., Lines 22, 16, 4; Ives, genealogical table, pg. xvii, 1986.

The Spear and the Spindle:
Ancestors of Sir Francis Bryan (d. 1550)
Bryan, Bourchier, Bohun, FitzAlan, and Others

Appendix B

Possible Ancestors and Descendants of Sir Francis Bryan

The genealogical table in this manuscript has been stopped at William de Bryan (RIN 1652) because of uncertainty on the part of your compiler. Although there is information concerning further ancestry of the Bryans, your compiler can find little, if any, reference to the parentage of this particular individual. Doubtless the information is available; it simply has not been seen by your compiler.

In searching for William de Bryan, your compiler has come across the information which is presented here by source. The sources may or may not be acceptable to some genealogists (and these sources vary on the information given), but the use of most any ancestral listing is helpful, as the researcher can often "come in by the back door," that is, research the other family names mentioned in the hope of locating pertinent information concerning the main object of the search. The listings given in this appendix are for that purpose. The spellings of names are given as they appear in the various sources.

According to MacKenzie

MacKenzie's *Colonial Families* (Vol. II, Bryant section, pgs. 150-151) offers the following line:

Engelbert I, Seigneur de Brienne (d. 990). He was the father of

Engelbert II, Seigneur de Brienne (d. 1055). He was the father of

Gautier I, 1068-1080, m. Eustachie de Bar-Sur-Seine. He was the father of

Erard I, Count de Brienne, 1104-1112, m. Alex de Roucé Ramerie. He was the father of

Gautier II, Count de Brienne (d. 1156). He was the father of

The Spear and the Spindle:
Ancestors of Sir Francis Bryan (d. 1550)
Bryan, Bourchier, Bohun, FitzAlan, and Others   **Appendix B**

Erard II, Count de Brienne (d. 1189), m. Agnes de Montbelliar*.
(Erard II's eldest son, Gauthier de Brienne, m. Alberic, daughter of
Tancréde, King of Sicily.) Erard II was the father of

Jean de Brienne (b. 1150, d. 23 Mar 1237 Constantinople) took part in
the 5th Crusade. He was "Holy King of Cypress and Jerusalem in Tyre
and later Emperor of the East (Constantinople), 1231-1237."
M. (1) 1209 Marie, daughter of Conrad and Isabelle de Monserrat,
heiress of the Kingdom of Jerusalem; m. (2) Berengaria, daughter of
Alphonso IX of Castile and Leon.** (See in this appendix, **Jean de
Brienne, King of Jerusalem.**) His eldest son by his second wife was

Alphonse de Brienne m. Mary, daughter and heiress of Ralph, Count of
Lusignan. Their younger son

Guy de "Brienne, Brion, Brian, or Bryan, Baron" [Compiler's note:
also seen spelled as Bryene] m. Lady Jane de la Pole. Their eldest son

Guy de Brian, Baron of Talacharn (d. 1307), m. Eva, daughter and
heiress of Henry de Tracy. Their eldest son

Sir Guy de Bryan, Baron of Chastel Walwyn, m. Sibil, daughter of
Walter de Sully. His eldest son

Guy de Bryan (d. 1347) was Baron of Chastel Walwyn, 1336. He
distinguished himself at Crecy in 1346; m. Anne, daughter of Hogan.
His eldest son

Lord Guy de Bryan (d. 1390), Baron Chevalier, was named Admiral of
the King's fleet in 1361 and elected 57th Knight of the Garter in 1370.

---

* According to Weis (Line 114), Erard II married in 1166 Agnes de Montfaucon, the
daughter of Richard II, Count of Montbéliard. Erard II was killed 8 Feb 1191 at Acre in the
3rd Crusade.
** According to Previte-Orton (Genealogical Table 22, where her ancestry is included),
Berengaria was a granddaughter of Eleanor (d. 1214) (daughter of Henry II of England) and her
husband Alfonso VIII of the House of Castile.

Appendix B

The Spear and the Spindle:
Ancestors of Sir Francis Bryan (d. 1550)
Bryan, Bourchier, Bohun, FitzAlan, and Others

He m. Elizabeth, daughter of William de Montacute, Earl of Salisbury*. MacKenzie says that their eldest son, Guy, died without male heirs.

Sir William de Bryan, Kt., (RIN 1652) (d. 20 Mar 1413) was the second son of Guy de Bryan and Elizabeth de Montacute. He married Joan (d. 1 Sep 1404), the daughter of John FitzAlan, 1st Lord Maltravers**.

The line is continued in the genealogical table of this manuscript. Briefly listed here:
Sir Thomas Bryan, eldest son, m. Margaret Echyngham and had
Sir Edmund Bryan, eldest son, m. Alice Bures and had
Sir Thomas Bryan, eldest son, m. Margaret Bowsey and had
Sir Thomas Bryan, eldest son, m. Margaret Bouchier and had
Sir Francis Bryan (d. 1550), "eldest son"***

According to Burke

According to *A Genealogical History of the Dormant, Abeyant, Forfeited, and Extinct Peerages of the British Empire* by Sir Bernard Burke (pg. 82), Guy de Brian, "whose chief seat was in the marches of Wales," m. (1) Eve, the only daughter and heiress of Henry de Traci. Guy and Eve had an only daughter, Maud, who married Nicholas Martin, Baron of Kemes. By his other wife, Guy left a son

Guy de Bryan, Baron of Chastel Walweyn. When he became of unsound mind, the barony was transferred to his son Guoyen, who was providing for his two sisters. This son

---

* The *CP*, Salisbury section, states that William (de Montague) (d. 30 Jan 1343/1344), Earl of Salisbury and Lord Montague, m. Katherine, youngest daughter of the three daughters of William (de Grandison), 1st Lord Grandison, by Sibyl, daughter and coheiress of John (Tregoz), Lord Tregoz. According to the *CP*, William and Katherine had, among others, Elizabeth Montacute, who m. (1) Giles (de Badlesmere), Lord Badlesmere; m. (2) Hugh le Despenser, Lord Despenser; m. (3) Guy (de Bryan), Lord Bryan.
** Weis (Line 59-35) agrees with this marriage but does not give the parents of William de Brien.
*** MacKenzie's words (Vol. II, pg. 151). Your compiler has seen no mention of other male issue of Sir Thomas Bryan and Margaret Bouchier; there were two daughters, Elizabeth and Margaret Bryan (see under Sir Francis Bryan in **Short Biographies** section).

The Spear and the Spindle:
Ancestors of Sir Francis Bryan (d. 1550)
Bryan, Bourchier, Bohun, FitzAlan, and Others   Appendix B

Guoyen de Bryan served under Edward III, was governor of
St. Briavel's Castle, was warden of the forest of Dene, co. Gloucester,
and was engaged in the French wars. He died 1350. His son

Guy de Bryan married Elizabeth de Montacute, daughter of William de
Montacute, Earl of Salisbury, and widow of Hugh le Despenser. This
Bryan was a Knight of the Garter, admiral of the king's fleet, and was
summoned as a baron to Parliament from 25 Nov 1350 to 6 Dec 1389.
[Compiler's note: At this time in my research, this is the only Guy de
Bryan seen thus far who was a K.G. He d. 1390.] Along with two
younger sons, who died issueless, he had*

Guy (d. 1368, in the lifetime of his father), who left two daughters

Philippa and Elizabeth. Burke adds, "His lordship d. in 1390, leaving
his two grand-daus., Philippa, then twelve, and Elizabeth, nine years of
age, his co-heirs, between whom the Barony of Bryan fell into
abeyance, and it became extinct, at the decease of Avice, countess of
Ormond, in 1456." [Compiler's remark: If Guy died in 1368, how
could his two daughters be the stated ages in 1390, the year their
grandfather died?] Burke continues: Philippa m. (1) John Devereux;
m. (2) Sir Henry le Scrope, Kt., "but d.s.p. 8th Henry IV," i.e., died
without issue about 1406. The other daughter, Elizabeth, m. Sir Robert
Lovell, Kt., and had Maud, an only child, who m. (1) John Fitzalan,
Earl of Arundel. They were parents of Humphrey, Earl of Arundel, who
died without issue; Maud m. (2) Sir Richard Stafford and had Avice,
who m. James Butler, Earl of Ormonde, and died without issue in
1456**. [Compiler's remark: Please see footnote.]

---

* Compilers's note: Burke does not mention a William. However, Burke's purpose here is to
trace the heirs to the barony.
** According to the *DNB* ["John VI FitzAlan, Earl of Arundel (1408-1435)"], Maud was the
second wife of the Earl of Arundel and the daughter of Robert Lovell. She was also "widow
of Sir R. Stafford." Their son Humphrey FitzAlan (1429-1438) succeeded his father in the
earldom, and Humphrey was succeeded by his uncle. The *CP*, Arundel section, says Maud
(d. 19 May 1436) was the widow of Sir Richard Stafford (d. abt 1427), that she was the
daughter of Robert Lovell, and that her mother Elizabeth was the daughter and coheiress "of
Sir Guy Bryene, who was 1st [son] and [heir apparent] of Sir Guy de Bryene [Lord
Bryene]." Maud m. (2) bef 1429 John Arundel, Lord Arundel, also Duke of Touraine in
France. Humphrey is listed as the only child of Lord Arundel and his second wife, having
been born 30 Jan 1429 and dying unmarried 24 Apr 1438 in his tenth year when "his
maternal inheritance, the property of the Bryene family, passed to his half sister, Avice

Appendix B

The Spear and the Spindle:
Ancestors of Sir Francis Bryan (d. 1550)
Bryan, Bourchier, Bohun, FitzAlan, and Others

Concerning a Philippa Brian

Browning's *Americans of Royal Descent* (Pedigree CI, pg. 452): "Sir Henry, third Lord Scrope, K.G., treasurer of England, beheaded in August, 1415; m. Lady Philippa, daughter of Sir Guy de Brian, K.G...." Sir Henry was a descendant of Edward I of England and his second queen, Margaret, daughter of Philip III, King of France. Issue listed for Sir Henry and Lady Philippa is Lady Jane le Scrope m. Henry, second Lord Fitzhugh, of Ravensworth, and had Lady Eleanor FitzHugh, sister of Sir Henry, Lord Fitzhugh (d. 1425), K.G.

Browning's *Magna Charta Barons 1898* (pg. 313) : "Sir Henry, third Baron, m. first, Philippa, daughter of Sir Guy de Brien, and had Lady Joan m. Henry Fitz-Hugh, second Baron...." They had Henry, third Baron, who had a Lady Eleanor.

Weis (6th ed., Line 219-33): Elizabeth de Marmion (d. Dec. 1427) m. Henry, Lord Fitz Hugh (b. abt 1358, d. 11 Jan 1424/25, Ravensworth), K.G., son of Henry Fitz Hugh by Joan, da. of Sir Henry Lescrope of Masham.

If this is the granddaughter Philippa mentioned above, these references differ from Burke (pg. 82 as above), who states that Philippa died without issue.

According to Thomas R. Bryan

According to Thomas Ray Bryan's *The Name and Family of Bryan or Brian* (pg. ix), Guy de Bryene and Elizabeth Montacute had "at least three sons, Sir Guy, Philip, and William Bryan, and possibly others as well." This book deals mostly with later American generations and the information on Guy and Elizabeth's issue was scanty, as presented.

According to Turton

Turton's *The Plantagenet Ancestry* (pgs. 119, 3) includes the following descendants (noted where Weis agrees) of Guy de Brien and Eva de Tracy who had

---

Stafford (b. 4 Dec 1423)." Avice m. James Butler, afterwards Earl of Wiltshire. [Compiler's note: According to the dates given in *CP*, Burke's listing of Maud's marriages is reversed.]

The Spear and the Spindle:
Ancestors of Sir Francis Bryan (d. 1550)
Bryan, Bourchier, Bohun, FitzAlan, and Others

Appendix B

Maude de Brien m. Sir Nicholas Martin and had

William, 1st Lord Martin, m. Eleanor, da. of Reynold/Reginald
FitzPiers and Joan Vivonia, (Weis, 6th ed., Line 122-32) and had

Joan Martin, widow of Henry Lacy, Earl of Lincoln, m. Nicholas
Audley (Weis, 6th ed., Line 122-32). Referring to Weis: Nicholas
Audley (b. 11 Nov 1289, m. 1312, d. Dec 1316), Lord Audley was a
descendant of William Longespee, illegitimate son of Henry II, King of
England. Joan and Nicholas had James Audley (b. 8 Jan 1312/13,
d. Apr 1386), K.G., m. (1) bef 13 Jun 1330 Joan Mortimer
(d. 1337/1351); Weis, 6th ed., Line 71: m. (2) by 1351 Isabel, "said to
be" the daughter of Roger, 5th Lord Strange of Knockyn. James Audley
had issue by both wives, but Weis does not list.

According to Stuart

Stuart's book includes some early counts of Brienne in his *Royalty for
Commoners* (Line 383).

Engelbert I, Count of Brienne, living 968, had

Engelbert II, Count of Brienne (d. abt 980), had

Engelbert III, Count of Brienne (d. bef 1035), had

Engelbert IV, Count of Brienne, (d. abt 1035), had

Walter I, Count of Brienne (d. abt 1089/90), m. Eustache de Bar-sur-
Seine, daughter of Milo I, Count of Bar-sur-Seine, and had

Milo II, Count of Bar-sur-Seine, living 1100 (d. 1125/26), had

Gui, Count of Bar-sur-Seine (d. 1145), m. Petronille of Chacenay
(d. 1161)

About Jean/John de Brienne, King of Jerusalem

Weis (6th ed., Line 114-28): Jean/John de Brienne (b. abt 1168,
d. 21 Mar 1237) was King of Jerusalem (1210-1215) and Emperor of
Constantinople (elected 1228). His father was Erard II, Count of
Brienne (killed in the 3rd Crusade at Acre, 8 Feb 1191), who

Appendix B

The Spear and the Spindle:
Ancestors of Sir Francis Bryan (d. 1550)
Bryan, Bourchier, Bohun, FitzAlan, and Others

m. 1166 Agnes de Montfaucon. She was the daughter of Richard II, Count of Montbéliard.

Jean de Brienne came to the throne of Jerusalem through the choice of Philip-Augustus of France. When the King of Jerusalem died, leaving no male issue, Jean de Brienne was chosen to marry the heiress. Harold Lamb, author of *The Flame of Islam*, (pg. 286) described Jean de Brienne as "an obscure knight...who lacked both wealth and rank, and who was not even young" but who had "a certain obstinate determination and a clear sense of honor...one of the ablest soldiers who ever wore the cross."

Jean de Brienne m. (1) 15 Sep 1210 Mary, daughter of Conrad de Montferrat and Isabel, daughter of Aumary I, King of Jerusalem. He ruled in right of his wife. After his wife died, leaving a daughter, Yolande, Jean de Brienne ruled in right of his daughter. He m. (2) 1214 Stephanie, daughter and heiress of Leo II, King of Armenia, but she died without issue 1219. After the marriage of his daughter, Yolande, he returned to Europe and m. (3) 1223 Berengaria of Leon (d. 12 Apr 1237), daughter of Alphonso IX, King of Castile and Leon*. By this third marriage was born (Weis, 6th ed., Line 114)

Louis de Brienne, Viscount of Beaumont in Maine, m. Agnes de Beaumont, daughter of Raoul, Viscount of Beaumont, and had

Henry de Beaumont (d. 10 Mar 1339/40), Lord Beaumont, Earl of Buchan, Justiciar of Scotland in 1338, m. abt 1310 Alice Comyn (d. bef 10 Aug 1349), daughter of Alexander Comyn by Joan**, sister of William le Latimer (Weis, 6th ed., Line 114A). Alexander Comyn was a descendant of Magna Charta Surety, Saher de Quency, and of Hugh Capet, King of France (Weis, 6th ed., Lines 114A, 53). Henry de Beaumont and Alice Comyn had

---

* *CP*, Beaumont section, contains a footnote stating that Alfonso IX was also the father of Ferdinand III, King of Castile and Leon. Ferdinand III was father of Eleanor (d. 1290) who married as his first wife Edward I, King of England.
** *CP*, Beaumont section, says "probably by Joan..."

The Spear and the Spindle:
Ancestors of Sir Francis Bryan (d. 1550)
Bryan, Bourchier, Bohun, FitzAlan, and Others

Appendix B

John de Beaumont (b. abt 1318, d. 10/25 May 1342) m. bef Jun 1337 Eleanor Plantagenet*, great-granddaughter of Henry III of England.

Lamb (pg. 286) says that Jean/John de Brienne was son of the Brienne who died at Acre and the brother of Walter [Compiler's note: also seen as Gautier] who served Innocent in Italy.

According to Lamb (pgs. 302-304), Yolande was married at age 13 to Frederick Hohenstaufen, son of Henry VI and Constance of Sicily, and a descendant of Frederick Redbeard. She lived in Brindisi Castle and died giving birth to her only child, Conrad. Lamb indicates the marriage was not a happy one for the young girl. He also states that Frederick, after his marriage to the heiress Yolande and his agreement to let Jean de Brienne continue ruling, then demanded that Jean de Brienne relinquish the rule of Jerusalem to him because Jean was not of noble blood and had no further right to rule. As above, this may be why Jean then returned to Europe.

According to Turton's *The Plantagenet Ancestry* (pgs. 167, 3) and to Weis (6th ed., Line 120): by his third marriage, Jean de Brienne also had

Jean de Brienne (d. 1296) m. Jeanne du Chateaudun and had

Blanche de Brienne (whom Weis calls Lady of Loupeland) m. Guillaume V (William) de Fiennes (*Sureties*, Line 147-4; CP IX, 281) and they became ancestors of, among others, Elizabeth Plantagenet (1465-1503, daughter of Edward IV and Elizabeth Woodville/Wydeville) (Turton, pgs. 167, 3) and Sir Thomas Boleyn (Weis, 6th ed., Line 120), father of Queen Anne Boleyn.

Descendants of Sir Francis Bryan (d. 1550)

The following listing of descendants is from MacKenzie's *Colonial Families* (Vol. II, Bryant section). At this writing, your compiler has not seen or sought these names elsewhere and has no further information on them. They are presented as possible working clues for the reader. The use of Esq. (Esquire) is interesting; this appellation denotes that the

---

* Daughter of Henry, Earl of Lancaster, and Maud (daughter of Sir Patrick Chaworth). Eleanor m. (2) 1345 Richard FitzAlan, Earl of Arundel "with whom she had intrigued in her husband's lifetime." She d. 11 Jan 1372 Arundel, bur. Lewes. (*CP*, Beaumont section).

Appendix B

The Spear and the Spindle:
Ancestors of Sir Francis Bryan (d. 1550)
Bryan, Bourchier, Bohun, FitzAlan, and Others

person was entitled to bear heraldic arms, a fact that might make tracing
an individual a little easier.

Sir Francis Bryan m. (1) Philippa, daughter of Sir John Montgomery.
"His son by first marriage" was

Edmund Brian of Tor Brian in Devon. His eldest son

Robert Bryan of Tor Brian, m. Eleanor, the daughter of Thomas
Bendish of Bumpstead. His eldest son

John Bryant of Tor Brian m. Rose. She was the daughter of John
Church of Erles, Colne, Co. Essex. His eldest son

John Bryant of Tor Brian m. Grace Wrayford. "He was ancestor of"

John Bryant of Bampton, Co. Devon. "Will proved 1641."

This line continues in *Colonial Families* to a Barbadoes immigrant.

Colonial Families (Vol. II) states that Sir Francis Bryan's son, Edmund
Brian, is the son of his first marriage. The *D.N.B.* ["Sir Francis Bryan
(d. 1550)"] states that Sir Francis Bryan married Philippa, heiress and
widow of Sir John Fortescue, after 1517; Philippa died after 1534.

In *Colonial Families* (Vol. VI, Bryan section) MacKenzie begins with
William Smith Bryan, a landholder in County Clare, Ireland, who was
transported to America (1650) and settled in Gloucester County,
Virginia. He had eleven sons, Morgan Bryan (liv. 1693 Norfolk Co.)
being "probably" one of the eleven, and Francis Bryan being the oldest.
Francis returned to Ireland (1677), sought unsuccessfully to recover his
inheritance of titles and estates, and fled to Denmark. Francis had a son
Morgan born in Denmark. Francis later returned to Ireland. MacKenzie
says "it is believed" that William Bryan (b. 1685) was also his
[Francis'] son. William Bryan m. Margaret and resided at Ballyroney,
County Down, Ireland. They had a son John. They sailed for America
in 1718.

Colonial Families (Vol. VI) continues, saying that the Morgan Bryan
born in Denmark m. Martha Strode. His brother, William (b. 1685
Ireland) as above m. Margaret. William and Margaret had John Andrew
(b. 1 May 1744), James, and William who m. Margaret Watson.

The Spear and the Spindle:
Ancestors of Sir Francis Bryan (d. 1550)
Bryan, Bourchier, Bohun, FitzAlan, and Others

Appendix B

John Andrew Bryan, as above (b. 1 May 1744, d. bet 9 Oct and 9 Dec 1779), served under Washington and in the Revolutionary War. He m. Mary Morrison and had William (b. 1 May 1744 [*sic*]) who m. Mary __; Andrew Morrison (b. 25 Apr 1748) who was in the Revolutionary War in Captain Leftwitch's Company; Mary (b. 27 May 1750) d. young; Margaret (b. 14 Mar 1752) who m. (1) David Mitchell, m. (2) Patrick Gibson; John (b. 19 Dec 1756) who also served in the Revolutionary War in Captain Leftwitch's Company, and m. Catherine Evans; Jane (b. 16 May 1761) who m. John Davison; Agnes (b. 9 Aug 1763) who m. (1) John Akers, m. (2) Reuben B. Bagby; Catherine (b. 21 Oct 1765) who m. Samuel Cole.

Andrew Morrison Bryan, son of John Andrew Bryan as above, (b. 25 April 1748, d. 20 April 1821) of Campbell Co., Virginia, m. Mary Akers (b. 15 Mar 1754, d. 17 Feb 1823) and had John (b. 4 Mar 1774) who m. Rebecca __; Elizabeth (b. 1 Jun 1776) who m. John Page; William Akers (b. 1 Oct 1778); Morrison (b. 14 Feb 1781); James (b. 23 Jun 1785, d. 19 Apr 1864) who m. Mary Johnson; Mary (b. 14 Jun 1787, d. 6 Sep 1839) who m. George Evans; Thomas (b. 25 Feb 1791, d. 6 Oct 1853) who m. Mary Bryan (d. 4 May 1852); David (b. 24 Oct 1793, d. 26 Feb 1881) who m. Mildred Johnson (d. 27 Feb 1881).

Colonial Families (Vol. VI, Bryan section) continues with issue of Morrison Bryan, as above, of Highland County, Ohio.

According to Whitfield

Whitfield's *Whitfield, Bryan, Smith and Related Families* (Vol. II, pgs. 157, 407-408) offers the following line:

Edmund Bryan, son of Sir Francis Bryan, m. Margaret Courtney. They lived at Tor Bryan in Devonshire.

Robert Bryan, Esq., (b. 1548) m. Elizabeth Livingston.

Thomas Bryan, Esq., m. (1) ?; (2) Margaret Compton. Lived in Aylesbury, Co. Buckingham.

Guy Bryan (b. 1601) m. Rebecca Kirkman. Lived at Aylesbury. Whitfield says he was a merchant. His son

Appendix B

The Spear and the Spindle:
Ancestors of Sir Francis Bryan (d. 1550)
Bryan, Bourchier, Bohun, FitzAlan, and Others

Josiah Bryan (b. 1634, d. 1685) m. Mary Longlands of
Co. Buckingham. Whitfield says he was a merchant and banker.

Edward Bryan (b. 1663 London, d. 1739), second son, m. Christianna
Council after immigrating to America abt 1690. She was daughter of
Hodges Council and Lucy Hardy/Hardee, daughter of John
Hardy/Hardee.

Whitfield lists issue of Edward and Christianna as William Bryan, John
Bryan, Lewis Bryan, and Hardy Council (?) Bryan [sic].

About Joan FitzGerald, Second Wife of Sir Francis Bryan

As stated in the Short Biographies section, Sir Francis Bryan
m. (2) 1548 Joan FitzGerald [D.N.B., "Sir Francis Bryan (d. 1550)"].
She was the daughter of James FitzMaurice (FitzGerald), the 10th Earl
of Desmond, and widow of James Butler, 9th Earl of Ormond and
Ossory. This James Butler, called "the Lame," died 28 Oct 1546,
London, from poison taken at a supper on Oct 17. His steward and
sixteen of his servants reportedly died of the same (CP, Ormond
section, pg. 144). It is interesting to note that not only did her first
husband die unpleasantly, Sir Francis Bryan died of unknown causes
while, it is said, Joan was seeing Gerald FitzJames (FitzGerald), 14th
Earl of Desmond, called "the Rebel Earl," who would, soon after Sir
Francis Bryan's death, become her third husband (m. 1550/1551)
(Chambers, Genealogical Table 2). There was no issue of the third
marriage. Joan died 2 Jan 1564/65 (CP, Desmond section, pg. 253).
There was no mystery about Gerald FitzGerald's death: for intriguing
against the English government, he was attainted, chased down, and on
11 Nov 1583 slain, and his head sent to Queen Elizabeth I (CP,
Desmond section, pg. 253; Berleth, pgs. 81, 296). The story is that
Elizabeth had it impaled on London Bridge (Berleth, pg. 204).

The information about Joan is offered for this reason: Thomas R. Bryan
in The Name and Family of Bryan or Brian (pg. ix) states that Sir
Francis Bryan had issue of a son named Francis by his second wife,
Joan, daughter of James FitzGerald, Earl of Desmond. Joan and Sir
Francis Bryan were married bef 28 Aug 1548, and he died 2 Feb
1549/1550 (CP, Ormond section, pg. 144).

This is a summary of one variation of the stories concerning the young
Francis Bryan (from the above mentioned The Name and Family): He
held lands in the County of Clare, Ireland; married an Ann Smith,

The Spear and the Spindle:
Ancestors of Sir Francis Bryan (d. 1550)
Bryan, Bourchier, Bohun, FitzAlan, and Others

Appendix B

daughter of Sir William Smith, and by her had a son William or William Smith Bryan, who was deported in 1650 by Cromwell. His son, Francis Bryan, returned to Ireland to claim his ancestral properties, failed, and moved on to Denmark where he married Sarah Brinker [Compiler's note: seen also as Brunker and Bringer]. After returning to Ireland, he died at Belfast in 1694, "leaving two sons, William and Morgan, both of whom emigrated to America in the early 18th century" (pg. x). It has been suggested that this Morgan could be the Morgan Bryan who married Martha Strode, moved to North Carolina, and together they became the ancestors of Rebecca Bryan, wife of Daniel Boone (Spraker's *The Boone Family*, pgs. 505-506). There were many other Bryan-Boone marriages as well (see Spraker, pg. 507).

Spraker (pg. 509) includes a typed copy of Joseph Bryan's will (probated in Jefferson County, Kentucky, 4 Mar 1805) in which he spells the names of his daughters, Martha and Rebecca, as *Boon*. *Boon* is actually the correct pronunciation of *Bohun*, a prominent family in medieval English history. Bakeless (pg. 3) writes, "Once, centuries earlier, they [the Boones] had been Bohuns, Normans." Bakeless adds (pg. 435, note 3.3), "The exact relationship of the Bohuns and Boones has never been established. No one doubts that it exists."

According to Edward A. Bryan

A similar story is contained in *Brianiana: A Biographical Pedigree* by Edward A. Bryan, 1934. [No title page accompanied the particular book—actually booklet—referenced by your compiler.] Sir Francis Bryan's son by Joan was Francis Bryan II (b. 1549) of County Clare, Ireland. He m. Ann, daughter of Sir William Smith, and had a son, William Smith Bryan, called "Prince William of Ireland" by his friends. "Prince William" attempted to claim the throne of Ireland during the Puritan rebellion and in 1650 was deported to Gloucester Beach, Virginia, by Cromwell.

Francis Bryan III, the oldest of his eleven sons, returned to Ireland to claim his hereditary estates but was so persecuted by the English government, he fled to Denmark. There he married Sarah Brinker, "a cousin of the Prince of Orange." In 1683, he returned to Ireland (d. 1694 Belfast). Francis Bryan III and Sarah Brinker had two sons, Morgan, b. 1671 in Denmark, and William, b. 1685 in Ireland. Both sons immigrated to America—Morgan in 1695 and William in 1718. The author says that William Jennings Bryan is a descendant of William.

Appendix B

The Spear and the Spindle:
Ancestors of Sir Francis Bryan (d. 1550)
Bryan, Bourchier, Bohun, FitzAlan, and Others

Morgan m. 1719 Martha Strode, "a descendant of Sir William Strode, one of the signers of the death warrant of Charles I." She was originally from Holland, and her parents were immigrating from France to flee religious persecution. Martha Strode's mother died at sea, leaving three children.

Morgan settled in Pennsylvania and in 1730 obtained a grant of land on the Potomac near Winchester, Virginia. Martha Strode died 1747. In 1748, he moved to the Yadkin River in North Carolina, near the present town of Wilkesboro. According to the author, members of the Bryan families of Virginia, North Carolina, and Kentucky are descendants of Morgan Bryan.

Bryan lists the children of Morgan Bryan and Martha Strode as Joseph, Eleanor, Mary, Samuel, Morgan, John, William, James, Thomas, Sarah, and Rebecca. William, James, and Morgan were involved with Daniel Boone and his expedition into Kentucky and the building of the fort of Bryan's Station.

The author offers his own lineage as follows:

Morgan Bryan m. Martha Strode and had

Morgan Bryan II m. a daughter of George Forbis and had

Joseph Bryan m. Ester Hampton and had

George Bryan m. Elizabeth Prewitt and had

Woodson Bryan m. Sophia Maddox and had

William Woodson Bryan m. Sophia Ewing and had

Roger Bryan m. Lucy Vaughan and had

Edward Bryan (the author of *Brianiana*)

The author does not list a wife for himself; he does, however, list the works consulted in the writing of his manuscript. They include *The Complete Peerage*, London, 1912; *O'Hart: Irish Pedigrees*, New York, 1923; Browning's *Americans of Royal Descent*, Philadelphia, 1894; *Dictionary of National Biography*, London, 1908; and others. He also mentions that various descendants can be found in Armstrong's *Notable*

The Spear and the Spindle:
Ancestors of Sir Francis Bryan (d. 1550)
Bryan, Bourchier, Bohun, FitzAlan, and Others   Appendix B

Southern Families; McKenzie's *Colonial Families of the U. S. A.*;
Cooper's *The Bryan Families of Fayette and Adjoining Counties*; and
Spraker's *The Boone Family*.

According to the author of *Brianiana*, Joan Fitzgerald, second wife of
Sir Francis Bryan (d. 1550) and mother of the young Sir Francis Bryan,
was through her mother, Amy (da. of Turlogh and Mor, da. of Donogh
O'Carroll), a descendant of King Brian, and through her father, James
Fitzmaurice Fitz-Gerald, "tenth Earl of Desmond," a descendant of the
Earls of Desmond.

According to Others

Several other books offer the story of the ancestors of Morgan Bryan,
and none give documentation. In fact, the Spraker book offers two of
the variations, one taken from a *Boone-Bryan History*, published by the
Kentucky State Historical Society, Frankfort, Kentucky; the second
"from a paper entitled 'Bryan Family, copied from the Biograph of
Dr. J. G. Bryan of St. Louis, Mo.,'" (Spraker, pg. 512). In both
instances, this is all the bibliographical information that is given.
Spraker admits that "neither account gives authority for statements."

In *Notable Southern Families* (Vol. II, Brian section) compiled by Zella
Armstrong, a lineage is given thus:

Francis Bryan [Compiler's note: Presumably the son of Joan FitzGerald
and Sir Francis Bryan (d. 1550)?] had William Smith Bryan (deported to
Gloucester Co., Virginia) who had eleven sons. Armstrong is sure of
the name of only the eldest—Francis (b. abt 1630). Francis returned to
Ireland in 1667 to claim his hereditary rights but had to flee to Denmark
where he married Sarah Brinker/Brunker. He died in Ireland 1694.
Francis had two sons, Morgan (b. Denmark 1671/81, d. 1763 aged
92 years) and William (b. Ireland 1685, m. Margaret). Morgan married
Martha Strode. Armstrong (Vol. II, pg. 34) remarks that though "all
family records" have a death date of 1747 in Virginia for Martha
Strode, "in Augusta County Records, Vol. III, p. 340, we find that on
September 27, 1753, Edward Hughes, Squire Boone and James Carter,
of Roane County, were appointed to take acknowledgement of Martha,
wife of Morgan Bryan." Morgan was buried in Rowan County. On
pg. 35, Armstrong notes that "His will on file at Salisbury County,
North Carolina, Will Book A, pg. 13." It mentions son Thomas,
daughter Elinor Linville, Joseph, Samuel, Morgan, John, William,
James and Thomas.

Appendix B

The Spear and the Spindle:
Ancestors of Sir Francis Bryan (d. 1550)
Bryan, Bourchier, Bohun, FitzAlan, and Others

Armstrong offers the issue (and their marriages) of Morgan Bryan and Martha Strode:

Joseph (b. 1720) m. (2) Hester Hampton "or name Alice and Hester" [*sic*].

Samuel m. Masmilla Simpson.

James m. 1756 Rebecca Knox.

Morgan Jr. (b. 20 May 1729) m. Mary Forbes.

John m. Frances Battle.

Elinor m. William Linville.

Mary m. Forbes.

William (d. 1781) m. 1755 Mary Boone, sister of Daniel Boone.

Thomas (b. 1736, d. 1789) m. ___ Hunt.

Sarah.

Rebecca m. 1755 Daniel Boone.

Armstrong (pg. 35) lists issue of the marriages and further descendants of the above in the same section, remarking that during the Revolutionary War, Samuel was the only son who who chose to fight for the King. He was later court-martialled and his property confiscated. Armstrong says there is no record of descendants for Samuel. However, Spraker (pg. 510) states that Samuel, son of Morgan Bryan and Martha Strode, eventually moved to New York, "where he left numerous descendants," and that "Samuel Bryan of Syracuse, N. Y., Congressman in 1902, a great grandson, had in his possession at one time the sword carried by his great-grandfather in the Revolutionary War."*

Spraker lists issue of Morgan Bryan and Martha Strode (pg. 508):

---

* Her footnote indicates her information is from a paper entitled "Bryan Family, copied from the Biograph of Dr. J. G. Bryan of St. Louis, Mo."

The Spear and the Spindle:
Ancestors of Sir Francis Bryan (d. 1550)
Bryan, Bourchier, Bohun, FitzAlan, and Others   Appendix B

Joseph Bryan, Sr. (d. abt 1805) m. (1) __; m. (2) Alee __.

Elenor/Ellender Bryan (d. abt 1792 Madison Co., Kentucky)
m. William Linville (d. 1766 killed by Indians).

Mary Bryan.

Samuel Bryan, fought for the British during the Revolutionary War.

Morgan Bryan m. __ Forbush, da. of George Forbush.

John Bryan.

William Bryan (b. 1733, d. 7 May 1780) m. abt 1755 Mary Boone,
sister of Daniel Boone.

James Bryan (d. abt 18 Aug 1807) m. 1756 Rebecca Enox/Enocks.

Thomas Bryan, "the youngest son," m. Sarah Hunt, da. of the
Rev. Jonathan Hunt, a descendant, Spraker says, of the first Episcopal
minister in Virginia, Robert Hunt, who had a church in Jamestown
1607.

Spraker adds the possibility of yet another child of Morgan Bryan and
Martha Strode as being Martha Bryan m. (1) Stephen Gano (Rowan
Co., N.C.); m. (2) __ Forbes/Forbis of Kentucky.

Note that Spraker (pg. 507) says that Rebecca Bryan, who married
Daniel Boone, was the daughter of Joseph Bryan, son of Morgan Bryan
and Martha Strode. She takes from the Draper ms a quote by
Col. Samuel Boone who remarked on "Joseph Bryan, the father-in-law
of Col. Daniel Boone..." (Spraker, pg. 509). This Joseph Bryan
(d. abt 1805) named Martha Boon and Rebecca Boon in his will as his
daughters. In his will he also mentions his wife Alee (who was his
second wife; the name of his first wife is not known, but Spraker notes
that Joseph Bryan, Jr., was her child); sons Samuel, Joseph, and John;
other daughters Mary Howard, Susannah Hinkle, Aylee Howard, Phebe
Forbis, Charity Davis, Elenor Adams; a granddaughter Aylee Adams;
grandsons Noah Adams, Jacob Adams, and Wilah Adams. The will was
dated 20 Nov 1804, witnessed by Edward Cox, Senior, David Enochs,
and Ephraim Hampton, and probated 4 Mar 1805.

Appendix B

The Spear and the Spindle:
Ancestors of Sir Francis Bryan (d. 1550)
Bryan, Bourchier, Bohun, FitzAlan, and Others

Spraker (pg. 509) lists the issue of Joseph Bryan of the above will and son of Morgan Bryan and Martha Strode:

Joseph Bryan Jr., "a half brother of Daniel Boone's wife."

Samuel Bryan.

John Bryan, "youngest son."

Martha Bryan m. Edward Boone (b. 19 Nov 1740, Exeter Township, Berks Co., Pa.; d. Oct 1780, killed by Indians).

Rebecca Bryan (b. 7 Feb 1739, d. 18 Mar 1813) m. Daniel Boone (b. 1734, d. 26 Sep 1820).

Mary Bryan m. __ Howard.

Susannah Bryan m. __ Hinkle.

Aylee Bryan m. __ Howard.

Phebe Bryan m. __ Forbis.

Charity Bryan m. __ Davis.

Elenor Bryan m. __ Adams.

Bryan-Council-Hardy Connection?

Armstrong (Vol. II, pg. 44) offers some descendants of a John O'Brien, who vied for the crown of Ireland and who "is said to be" a son of William Smith Bryan who was deported to the Virginia Colony in 1650 (pg. 33; she references McKenzie's *Colonial Families*, Vol. VI, as condensed above). Armstrong lists five sons of John O'Brien who immigrated to America, landing in New Berne before 1700: Edward (the eldest), John, William, Hardy, and Council (he died at sea; on the trip to America?). Armstrong says they dropped the *O* and spelled their name as *Bryan*. Edward (d. 1746) m. Anne/Ann and had John Bryan (d. 25 May 1801 Jones Co., N.C.), eldest son, who was a Colonel in the Revolutionary War "(D. A. R. Lineage Book, Vol. IX, p. 320)" (Armstrong, Vol. II, pg. 45).

The Spear and the Spindle:
Ancestors of Sir Francis Bryan (d. 1550)
Bryan, Bourchier, Bohun, FitzAlan, and Others   Appendix B

Your compiler cannot refrain from remarking on the unusual names of brothers Hardy and Council. Reference Whitfield's listing above of descendants of Sir Francis Bryan (d. 1550) and his first wife, Philippa Montgomery: Edward Bryan m. Christianna Council. From other sources it is believed that the Council, Hardy, and Bryan families were related by various marriages. Armstrong notes, "the name Hardy shows some connection with the O'Brien line (Vol. II, pg. 52)."

A line for a Hardy-Council-Bryan connection is given thus:

John Hardy (b. England 1613, d. Virginia 1670) m. Olivia/Olive Council/Councill and had

John Hardy (b. 1637, d. abt 1677) m. Alice Bennett Johnson and had

Lucy Hardy/Hardee m. 1666 Hodges Council/Councill (b. 1643, d. abt 1699) and had

Christiana Council (b. abt 1668, d. 1737) m. 1690 Edward Bryan (b. 1663, d. 1737/39) and had

John Bryan (b. 2 Jan 1692, d. 31 Oct 1741) m. unknown and had

Elizabeth Bryan (b. abt 1741/44, d. 18 Jun 1811) m. abt 1754 Richard Hart (b. 1719/20, d. abt 1783) and had

(the source of the above is Wurts' *Magna Charta*; the continuing line is a DAR-approved line)

John Bryan Hart, Revolutionary War Service, (b. abt 1760, d. bef 1830) m. abt 1781 Mary Gill (b. abt 1759, d. abt 1820) (daughter of John Gill, Revolutionary War soldier) and had

Mary Hart (b. 9 Oct 1790, d. 1822) m. abt 1808 Joseph Price, Sr. (b. 7 July 1785, d. 30 Sep 1875) and had

Joseph Price, Jr. (b. 7 Nov 1821, d. 2 Oct 1878) m. 11 Jan 1844 Elizabeth Raiburn/Raiborn (b. 1827, d. 15 Sep 1878) and had

John Lewis Price (b. 5 Sep 1854, d. 14 Feb 1922) m. 17 Dec 1882 Elizabeth Lenora McGrew (b. 13 Mar 1866, d. 7 Oct 1942) and had

Appendix B

The Spear and the Spindle:
Ancestors of Sir Francis Bryan (d. 1550)
Bryan, Bourchier, Bohun, FitzAlan, and Others

Joseph Duncan Price (b. 19 Aug 1889, d. 10 Oct 1968) m. 22 Apr 1922 Bertie Mae Harrell (b. 17 Oct 1903, d. 10 Jun 1984) and had

Martha Elizabeth Price (b. 26 Dec 1923) m. 9 Jun 1945 Grady Webster Leese (b. 16 Sep 1921).

Your compiler wishes there were more facts in hand to offer concerning the Bryan-Council-Hardy connection.

Note that the mention of the above books is no more than that. The information and names from the books are included here in case the reader would like to do some whole family research based on the many family names and information given. Your compiler's research deals mostly with earlier times.

The Spear and the Spindle:
Ancestors of Sir Francis Bryan (d. 1550)
Bryan, Bourchier, Bohun, FitzAlan, and Others

Appendix B

The Spear and the Spindle:
Ancestors of Sir Francis Bryan (d. 1550)
Bryan, Bourchier, Bohun, FitzAlan, and Others

Appendix C

"A Time When Christ and His Saints Slept"

The story of the rivalry between Stephen and his cousin the Empress
Matilda (RIN 207) for the crown of England might be considered a
romantic and colorful episode in the pageant of English history had not
it had such a devastating effect on the country. In reality, it was a
family feud that affected and infected the country with lawlessness,
starvation, cruelty, and death. And those that suffered the most were the
innocent common people.

The Empress Matilda (she was widow of the German Emperor
Henry V) was the only surviving legitimate issue of Henry I (RIN 210),
King of England, and his queen, Matilda of Scotland (RIN 211). As
such, she had been chosen by her father as heir to his throne. Three
times he had had the barons swear to accept and support her as their
ruler. Yet when Henry died on 1 Dec 1135, the Empress Matilda's
cousin, Stephen of Blois (one of those who had promised to accept her
as Henry's heir), hurried to England and laid claim to the crown, saying
he was Henry's favorite nephew and grandson of William the
Conqueror. Stephen was a charming and gallant man, and the people of
London accepted him. Many of the barons decided to support him and
broke their oaths, saying that the oaths had been extracted from them
against their will and, furthermore, they did not want to be ruled by a
woman. So Stephen was crowned King of England at Christmastime
1135 in Westminster Abbey.

In 1139, the Empress Matilda, supported by the barons who honored
their oaths to Henry, arrived in England to challenge Stephen, and for
the remainder of Stephen's reign there was civil war in England between
the two factions. Because the King was too involved in defending his
throne, he had no time or resources to maintain the laws of the land,
and men made their own laws, robbed, abused, and killed their
neighbors, tortured passersby for the little gold they might be carrying,
and in general wreaked havoc across the country. Livestock and crops
were stolen or destroyed, and people starved. As charming as Stephen
might have been, he proved an inept and ineffectual ruler. His queen,
Matilda of Boulogne, was a great aid to him and served as leader of his
army when he was captured by the Empress Matilda. Queen Matilda
negotiated for his release, and the Empress Matilda, who actually had
the victory (and the crown) in her pocket, agreed (for whatever reason)

119

The Spear and the Spindle:
Ancestors of Sir Francis Bryan (d. 1550)
Bryan, Bourchier, Bohun, FitzAlan, and Others

Appendix C

to return the queen's husband to her in exchange for her own illegitimate half-brother and commander, Robert, Earl of Gloucester.

The story reads like a game of chess, the king and queen being cornered or captured, being protected by the knights, the chase continuing, and the common people, like pawns, being sacrificed in the struggle to win the contest for the crown.

The Empress Matilda lost her commander, Robert, and retired to Normandy, and her son Henry (now 21, who had been two years old when Stephen was crowned) crossed to England to state his claim to the throne. In 1153, the Treaty of Westminster was signed, by which it was agreed that Stephen would continue to rule until his death and that the Empress Matilda's son, Henry, would be his heir to the throne.

The following year, on 25 Oct 1154, Stephen died, ending a reign that had been described in the *Anglo-Saxon Chronicle* as a time when "Christ and his saints slept." Henry succeeded with no opposition and in Westminster Abbey on 19 Dec 1154 was crowned Henry II.

The first years of Henry II's reign were spent in restoring peace to England. The Empress Matilda stayed in Normandy, living near Rouen. Her last 13 years were spent in good works: she founded several religious houses, was a benefactress to hospitals, churches, and monasteries, and in her last will arranged for a distribution of her wealth to the poor. (*D.N.B.*, "Matilda, Maud, Mold, Aethelic, Aaliz (1102-1167)"; *KQB*, pgs. 50-53)

The table illustrates the family connections among the principle players in the wars of Stephen's reign.

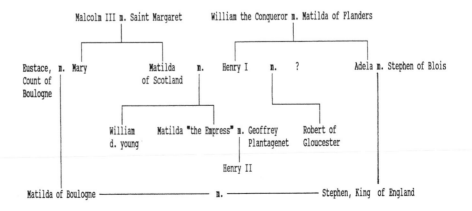

The Spear and the Spindle:
Ancestors of Sir Francis Bryan (d. 1550)
Bryan, Bourchier, Bohun, FitzAlan, and Others

Appendix D

List of Sureties for the Magna Charta

The seventeen Sureties known to have descendants living to the present day:

<u>RIN</u>

1138		William d'Albini, Lord of Belvoir Castle, Leicestershire, d. 1236
202		Roger Bigod, Earl of Norfolk (and Suffolk?), d. 1220
177	*	Hugh Bigod, son of Roger Bigod, d. 1225
247	*	Henry de Bohun, Earl of Hereford, d. 1220
362	*	Richard de Clare, Earl of Hertford, d. 1217
367	*	Gilbert de Clare, son of Richard de Clare, d. 1230.
405		John FitzRobert, Lord of Warkworth Castle, Northumberland, d. 1240
		Robert FitzWalter, Lord of Dunmow Castle, Essexshire, d. 1234
		William de Huntingfield, a feudal baron in Suffolk, d. 1220
356	*	John de Lacie, Lord of Halton Castle, Cheshire, d. 1240
		William de Lanvallei, Lord of Stanway Castle, Essex, d. 1217
344		William Malet, Lord of Curry-Malet, Somersetshire, d. abt 1217
		William de Mowbray, Lord of Axholme Castle, Lincolnshire, d. 1223
128	*	Saire de Quincey, Earl of Winchester, d. 1219
1142		Robert de Roos, Lord of Hamlake Castle, Yorkshire, d. 1226
		Geoffrey de Saye, a feudal baron in Sussex?, d. 1230
137	*	Robert de Vere, Earl of Oxford, d. 1221

(*MC*, pgs. 30-31)

* Denotes that this Surety is present in this manuscript.

The Spear and the Spindle:
Ancestors of Sir Francis Bryan (d. 1550)
Bryan, Bourchier, Bohun, FitzAlan, and Others

Appendix D

The Spear and the Spindle:
Ancestors of Sir Francis Bryan (d. 1550)
Bryan, Bourchier, Bohun, FitzAlan, and Others

Appendix E

Kings of England and Dates of Reign (1066-1547)

The Normans

1066-1087	William I the Conqueror
1087-1100	William II Rufus
1100-1135	Henry I
1135-1154	Stephen (contested by Matilda "the Empress")

The Plantagenets

1153-1189	Henry II
1189-1199	Richard I
1199-1216	John
1216-1272	Henry III
1272-1307	Edward I
1307-1327	Edward II
1327-1377	Edward III
1377-1399	Richard II

The House of Lancaster

1399-1413	Henry IV
1413-1422	Henry V
1422-1461	Henry VI

The House of York

1461-1483	Edward IV
1483	Edward V
1483-1485	Richard III
1485-1509	Henry VII
1509-1547	Henry VIII

The Spear and the Spindle:
Ancestors of Sir Francis Bryan (d. 1550)
Bryan, Bourchier, Bohun, FitzAlan, and Others

Appendix E

The Spear and the Spindle:
Ancestors of Sir Francis Bryan (d. 1550)
Bryan, Bourchier, Bohun, FitzAlan, and Others

List of Abbreviations

b.	born
bur.	buried
CP	*Complete Peerage* by Cokayne
d.	died
D.N.B.	*Dictionary of National Biography*
div.	divorced
ex.	executed
Enc. Brit.	*Encyclopedia Britannia*
KQB	*DeBrett's Kings and Queens of Britain* by Williamson
KQE	*DeBrett's Kings and Queens of Europe* by Williamson
Kt.	Knight
m.	married
MC	*Magna Charta* by John Wurts
RIN	Record Identification Number
MRIN	Marriage Record Identification Number
Sureties	*The Magna Charta Sureties, 1215* by Weis and Adams
unm.	unmarried
Weis, 6th ed.	*Ancestral Roots of Sixty Colonists* by Weis

Abbreviations frequently encounter in research

d.s.p.	died without issue
d.s.p.l.	died without legitimate issue
d.s.p.m.	died without male issue
d.s.p.m.s.	died without surviving male issue
d.s.p.s.	died without surviving issue
d.v.p.	died in the lifetime of the father
d.v.m.	died in the lifetime of the mother

The Spear and the Spindle:
Ancestors of Sir Francis Bryan (d. 1550)
Bryan, Bourchier, Bohun, FitzAlan, and Others

Abbreviations

The Spear and the Spindle:
Ancestors of Sir Francis Bryan (d. 1550)
Bryan, Bourchier, Bohun, FitzAlan, and Others

Bibliography and References

History Today Magazine, April 1990

History Today Magazine, July 1991

Westminster Abbey: Official Guide, Jarrold and Sons Limited, Norwich, 1988

Adams, Arthur, and Weis, F. L., *The Magna Charta Sureties, 1215*, Genealogical Publishing Co., Inc., Baltimore, MD, 1964

Addison, William, *Essex Worthies*, Phillomore & Co. Ltd., London and Chichester, 1973

Alderman, Clifford Lindsey, *Blood-Red the Roses*, Julian Messner, NY, 1971

Appleby, John T., *Henry II: The Vanquished King*, G. Bell & Sons, Ltd., London, 1962

Armstrong, Zella, Comp., *Notable Southern Families*, The Lookout Publishing Co., Chattanooga, Tenn., 1922

Arnstein, Walter L., *Britain Yesterday & Today: 1830-Today*

Ashley, Maurice, *The Life and Times of King John*, Weidenfeld and Nicolson, London, 1972

Bagley, J. J., *The Earls of Derby 1485-1985*, Sidgwick & Jackson, London, 1985

Bakeless, John, *Daniel Boone: Master of the Wilderness*, William Morrow & Company, NY, 1939

Barlow, Frank, *Edward the Confessor*, University of California Press, Berkeley, Los Angeles, 1970

Barton, John and Law, Joy, *The Hollow Crown*, The Dial Press, NY, 1971

Belloc, Hilaire, *William the Conqueror*, Peter Davies Limited, Edinburgh, 1933

Bennett, Michael, *Lambert Simnel and the Battle of Stoke*, St. Martin's Press, NY, 1987

Berleth, Richard, *The Twilight Lords: An Irish Chronicle*, Alfred A. Knopf, NY, 1978

Besant, Walter, *Story of King Alfred*, D. Appleton and Company, 1902

Bingham, The Hon. Clive D., *The Chief Ministers of England 920-1720*, E. P. Dutton and Co., NY, 1923

Bingham, The Hon. Clive D., *The Marriages of the Bourbons*, Vol. 1, AMS Press, New York, 1970

Bingham, Caroline, *Kings and Queens of Scotland*, Dorset Press, NY, 1976

Boddie, John Bennett, *Virginia Historical Genealogies*, Genealogical Publishing Co., Inc., Baltimore, MD, 1965

Browning, Charles H., *The Magna Charta Barons and their American Descendants together with the Pedigrees of the Founders of the Order of Runnemede deduced from the Sureties for the Enforcement of the Statues of the Magna Charta of King John, 1898*, (reprinted 1991 by Genealogical Publishing Company, Inc., Baltimore, MD, for Clearfield Company, Inc.)

Browning, Charles H., *Americans of Royal Descent*, first edition 1883, seventh edition of 1911 reprinted by Genealogical Publishing Co., Inc., Baltimore, MD, 1986

Bruce, Marie Louise, *Anne Boleyn: A Biography*, Coward, Mccann & Geoghegan, Inc., NY, 1972

Bryan, Thomas R., *The Name and Family of Bryan or Brian*, Compiled by the Media Research Bureau, Washington, D.C., Shaffer Printing Co., Edgefield, SC, 1970

The Spear and the Spindle:
Ancestors of Sir Francis Bryan (d. 1550)
Bryan, Bourchier, Bohun, FitzAlan, and Others   **Bibliography and References**

Buck, Sir George, Ed., Kincaid, Arthur, *The History of King Richard the Third (1619)*, Alan Sutton, Gloucester, 1979

Burke, Sir Bernard, D.B., LL.D., *A Genealogical History of the Dormant, Abeyant, Forfeited, and Extinct Peerages of the British Empire*, (distributed by Heraldic Book Company, Baltimore), London, 1883

Burke, Esq., John, *Extinct and Dormant Baronetcies of England, Ireland, and Scotland*, Genealogical Publishing Co., Inc., London and Baltimore, 1985

Burke, John, *Life in the Castle in Medieval England*, Dorset Press, NY, 1978

Burke, John Bernard, Esq., *Roll of Battle Abbey*, Genealogical Publishing Co., Inc., Baltimore, MD, 1985

Canning, John, Ed., *100 Great Kings, Queens, and Rulers of the World*, Taplinger Publishing Co., NY 1968

Cannon, John and Griffiths, Ralph, *The Oxford Illustrated History of the British Monarchy*, Oxford University Press, Oxford and NY, 1988

Carpenter, Edward and Gentleman, David, *Westminster Abbey*, Weidenfeld and Nicolson, London, 1987

Chamberlin, Russel, *The Tower of London: An Illustrated History*, Webb & Bower Limited, 1987

Chambers, Anne, *Eleanor, Countess of Desmond*, Wolfhound Press, Dublin, 1986

Chapman, Hester, *The Sisters of Henry VIII*

Chapman, Hester W., *The Last Tudor King: A Study of Edward VI*, The MacMillan Company, New York, 1959

Chapman, Hester W., *The Challenge of Anne Boleyn*, Coward, Mccann & Geoghegan, Inc., NY, 1974

Chapman, Hester W., *Two Tudor Portraits: Henry Howard & Lady Katherine Grey*, Little, Brown and Company, Boston, Toronto, 1960

Chrimes, Ross, Griffiths, Eds., *Fifteenth Century England 1399-1509*, Manchester University Press, NY, 1972

Chrimes, S. B., *Lancastrians, Yorkists, & Henry VII*, MacMillan & Co Ltd, NY, St Martin's Press, 1964

Chute, Marchette, *Geoffrey Chaucer of England*, E. P. Dutton and Co., Inc., NY, 1946

Chute, Marchette, *Geoffrey Chaucer of England*, E. P. Dutton and Co., Inc., NY, 1958

Clifford, Esther Rowland, *A Knight of Great Renown*, The University of Chicago Press, 1961

Clive, Mary, *This Sun of York: A Biography of Edward IV*, Alfred A. Knopf, NY, 1974

Coffman, Ramon P., *Famous Kings and Queens for Young People*, A. S. Barnes & Company, NY, 1947

Cokayne, G. E., The Complete Peerage, St Catherine Press, London

Collins, *The Peerage of England*

Collis, Louise, *Memoirs of a Medieval Woman*, Harper & Row, NY,1964

Costain, Thomas B., *The Conquerors* (The Pageant of England Series), Doubleday & Company, Inc., Garden City, NY, 1949

Bibliography and References

The Spear and the Spindle:
Ancestors of Sir Francis Bryan (d. 1550)
Bryan, Bourchier, Bohun, FitzAlan, and Others

Costain, Thomas B., *The Magnificent Century*, Doubleday & Co., Inc., 1951

Costain, Thomas B., *The Three Edwards*

Thomas B., *The Last Plantagenets*, Popular Library Eagle Books Edition, NY, 1962

Daniell, Christopher, *A Traveller's History of England*, Interlink Books, NY, 1991

De Castries, Duc, *The Lives of the Kings & Queens of France*, Alfred A. Knopf, New York, 1979

Delderfield, Eric R., *Kings and Queens of England and Great Britain*, Taplinger Publishing Co., NY, 1970

Donaldson, Gordon, *Scottish Kings*, Barnes & Noble Books, NY, 1967

Douglas, David C., *William the Conqueror*, University of California Press, Berkeley & L. A., 1964

Duby, Georges, *William Marshal: The Flower of Chivalry*, Pantheon Books, NY, 1984, translation copyright 1985 by Richard Howard

Durant, Will, *The Age of Faith*, Simon and Schuster, NY, 1950

Ellis, Sir Geoffrey, Bt., *Earldoms in Fee*, The Saint Catherine Press, Limited, London, 1963

Elton, G. R., *England Under the Tudors*, Methuen & Co., Ltd, London, 1955

Erickson, Carolly, *Bloody Mary: The Remarkable Life of Mary Tudor*, Doubleday & Company, Inc., Garden City, NY, 1978

Erickson, Carrolly, *The First Elizabeth*, Summit Books, NY, 1983

Ferguson, John, *English Diplomacy 1422-1461*, Oxford at the Clarendon Press, 1972

Forester, Thomas, Ed. and Trans., *The Chronical of Henry of Huntingdon*, Henry G. Bohn, York St., Covent Garden, 1853

Fraser, Antonia, *The Warrior Queens*, Alfred A. Knopf, NY, 1989

Fry, Plantagenet Somerset, *The Tower of London: Cauldron of Britain's Past*, Quiller Press, London, 1990

Fuller, Thomas & Freeman, *The Worthies of England*, George Allen & Unwin John Ltd, London, 1952

Fuller, Thomas, *Fuller's Worthies of England*, Vol II, AMS

D. D. Nuttall, P. Austin Press Inc., NY, 1965

Gairdner, James, *Houses of Lancaster and York*, Logmans, Green, and Co., 1887

Gardner, John, *The Life and Times of Chaucer*, Alfred A. Knopf, New York, 1977

Gascoigne, Christina and Bamber, *Castles of Britain*, Thames and Hudson, NY, 1992

Given-Wilson, Chris & Curteis, Alice, *The Royal Bastards of Medieval England*, Routledge and Kegan Paul, London, 1984

Goff, John, *We Never Could Say Their Names: An Account of the Camfield Family of Northamptonshire*, 1975

Green, John Richard, LL.D., *England*, Vol. I, Co-Operative Publication Society, NY, London

Green, Mary Anne Everett, *Lives of the Princesses of England*, Vols I-III, Henry Colburn, Pub., London, 1849

The Spear and the Spindle:
Ancestors of Sir Francis Bryan (d. 1550)
Bryan, Bourchier, Bohun, FitzAlan, and Others   Bibliography and References

Griffiths, Ralph A., *The Reign of King Henry VI*, Ernest Benn Limited, London, Kent, 1981

Grimble, Ian, *The Harington Family*, Jonathan Cape, London, 1957

Grinnell-Milne, Duncan, *The Killing of William Rufus: An Investigation in the New Forest*, Augustus M. Kelley Publishers, NY, 1968

Hackett, Francis, *Henry the Eighth*, Garden City Publishing Co., Inc., Garden City, NY, 1929

Haigh, Christopher, *The Reign of Elizabeth I*, MacMillan, 1984

Hallam, Elizabeth, Ed., *The Plantagenet Encyclopedia*, Grove Weidenfeld, NY, 1990

Hallam, Elizabeth, Ed., *The Plantagenet Chronicles*, Weidenfeld & Nicolson, NY, 1986

Hallam, Elizabeth, Ed., *The Wars of the Roses*, Weidenfeld & Nicholson, NY, 1988

Hallam, Elizabeth, Ed., *Four Gothic Kings*, Weidenfeld & Nicolson, NY, 1987

Harris, Barbara J. *Edward Stafford: Third Duke of Buckingham, 1478-1521*, Stanford University Press, Stanford, CA., 1986

Harvey, John, *The Plantagenets*, London, 1948

Hibbert, Christopher, *The Court at Windsor: A Domestic History*, Harper & Row, NY and Evanston, 1964

Hibbert, Christopher, *The Tower of London*, Newsweek, NY, 1971

Hicks, M. A., *False, Fleeting, Perjur'd Clarence, 1449-78*, Alan Sutton, 1980

Hollister, C. Warren, *The Making of England 55 B.C. to 1399*, D. C. Heath & Co., Lexington, Mass., 1966

Hutchinson, Harold F., *King Henry V*, The John Day Co., NY, 1967

Ives, Eric W., *Anne Boleyn*, Basil Blackwell, 1986

James, John, *The Traveler's Key to Medieval France*, Alfred A. Knopf, NY, 1986

Jenkins, Elizabeth, *Elizabeth the Great*, Coward-McCann, Inc., NY, 1959

Jenkins, Elizabeth, *The Princes in the Tower*, Coward, McCann & Geoghegan, Inc., NY, 1978

Jenner, Heather, *Royal Wives*, Gerald Duckworth & Co., Ltd., London, 1967

Joelson, Annette, *England's Princes of Wales*, Dorset Press, NY, 1966

Johnson, P. A., *Duke Richard of York 1411-1460*, Clarendon Press, Oxford, 1988

Jolliffe, John, Ed., *Froissart's Chronicles*, The Modern Library, NY, 1967

Kelly, Amy, *Eleanor of Aquitaine and the Four Kings*, Harvard University Press, Cambridge, Mass., 1950

Kendall, Paul Murray, *Warwick the Kingmaker*, W. W. Norton & Co., Inc., 1957

Kendall, Paul Murray, *Richard the Third*, W. W. Norton & Co., Inc., NY, 1955

Kerr, Nigel and Mary, *A Guide to Medieval Sites in Britain*, Paladin Grafton Books, London, 1989

Labarge, Margaret Wade, *Henry V*, Stein and Day Publishers, NY, 1976

Lamb, Harold, *The Flame of Islam*, Doubleday & Company, Inc., NY 1931

Lander, J. R., *Crown and Nobility, 1450-1509*, McGille-Queen's University Press, Montreal, 1976

Bibliography and References

The Spear and the Spindle:
Ancestors of Sir Francis Bryan (d. 1550)
Bryan, Bourchier, Bohun, FitzAlan, and Others

Lewis, Brenda Ralph, *Kings and Queens of England*, Ladybird Books, Loughborough, Leicestershire, UK, 1986

Littleton, Taylor & Rea, Robert R., *To Prove a Villain: The Case of King Richard III*, MacMillan Co., 1964

Lloyd, Alan, *The Making of the King: 1066*, Holt, Rinehart and Winston, NY, 1966

Loades, David, *Mary Tudor: A Life*, Basil Blackwell Ltd, Oxford, UK, Cambridge, Mass., 1989

Lofts, Norah, *Queens of England*, Doubleday & Company, Inc., Garden City, NY, 1977

Lofts, Norah, *Anne Boleyn*, Coward, Mccann & Geoghegan, Inc., NY, 1979

Loyn, H. R., Ed., *The Middle Ages: A Concise Encyclopedia*, Thames & Hudson, 1991

Macaulay, David, *Castle*, Houghton Mifflin, Boston, 1977

MacKenzie, George Norbury, Ed., *Colonial Families of the United States*, Genealogical Publishing Co., Inc., Baltimore, MD, 1966

Matthew, Gervase, *The Court of Richard II*, John Murray, 1968

Meade, Marion, *Eleanor of Aquitaine*, Hawthorn Books Publishers, Inc., NY, 1977

Michell, John, *The Traveler's Key to Sacred England*, Alfred A. Knopf, NY, 1988

Moncreiffe of That Ilk, Sir Iain, *Royal Highness: Ancestry of the Royal Child*, Hamish Hamilton, London, 1982

Mondadori, Arnoldo, Ed., *The Life and Times of Charlemagne*, The Danbury Press, Grolier Enterprises, Inc., 1972

Montague-Smith, Patrick W., *The Royal Line of Succession*, Pitkin Pictorials Ltd, London, 1968

Montague-Smith, Patrick W., *The Royal Line of Succession*, Pitkin Pictorials Ltd, London, 1972

Morgan, Kenneth O., *The Oxford Illustrated History of Britain*, Oxford University Press, Oxford, NY, 1986

Morris, Jean, *The Monarchs of England*, Charterhouse, NY, 1975

Murray, Jane, *The Kings and Queens of England: A Tourist Guide*, Charles Scribner's Sons, NY, 1974

Norgate, Kate, *Minority of Henry III*, London, 1912

Oman, Charles, *Castles*, Kelly & Kelly, Ltd, London, 1926

Packard, Jerrold M., *The Queen & Her Court*, Charles Scribner's Sons, NY, 1981

Pain, Nesta, *Empress Matilda, Uncrowned Queen of England*, Weidenfeld and Nicolson, London, 1978

Painter, Sidney, *William Marshal: Knight-Errant, Baron, and Regent of England*, University of Toronto Press, Toronto, 1982

Palmer, Alan, *Princes of Wales*, Weidenfeld and Nicolson, London, 1979

Phillips, J. R. S., *Aymer de Valence, Earl of Pembroke, 1307-1324*, Oxford at the Clarendon Press, 1972

Piper, David, *Kings & Queens of England and Scotland*, The Leisure Circle Limited, Middlesex, 1980

Plaidy, Jean, *The Queen from Provence*, G. P. Putnam's Sons, NY, 1981

The Spear and the Spindle:
Ancestors of Sir Francis Bryan (d. 1550)
Bryan, Bourchier, Bohun, FitzAlan, and Others   **Bibliography and References**

Plaidy, Jean, *The Passionate Enemies*, G. P. Putnam's Sons, NY, 1976

Plaidy, Jean, *The Lion of Justice*, G. P. Putnam's Sons, NY, 1979

Plaidy, Jean, *The Vow on the Heron*, Fawcett, Ballantine Books, NY, 1980

Plaidy, Jean, *The Bastard King*, G. P. Putnam Sons, NY, 1974

Plaidy, Jean, *Passage to Pontefract*, Fawcett, Ballantine Books, NY, 1981

Plaidy, Jean, *St. Thomas's Eve*, G. P. Putnam's Sons, New York, 1970

Plaidy, Jean, *The King's Pleasure*, Appleton-Century-Crofts, Inc., New York, 1949

Plaidy, Jean, *The King's Pleasure*, Appleton-Century-Crofts, Inc., NY, 1929

Plowden, Alison, *Tudor Women*, Atheneum, NY, 1979

Plowden, Alison, *Elizabeth Tudor and Mary Stewart: Two Queens in One Isle*, Barnes & Noble Books, Totowa, New Jersey, 1984

Plowden, Alison, *The Young Elizabeth*, Stein and Day Publishers, NY, 1971

Plowden, Alison, *The House of Tudor*, Stein and Day, New York, 1976

Plumb, J. H. and Wheldon, Huw, *Royal Heritage: The Treasures of the British Crown*, Harcourt Brace Jovanovich, 1977

Previte-Orton, C. W., *The Shorter Cambridge Medieval History*, The University Press, Cambridge, 1962

Radford, L. B., *Henry Beaufort*, 1908

Ramsay, J. H., *Lancaster and York*, Vol II 1437-1485, Oxford at the Clarendon Press, 1892

Ramsay, Sir J. H., *Lancaster and York*, Vol I 1399-1437, Oxford at the Clarendon Press, 1892

Reeves, A. C., *Lancastrian Englishmen*

Riley-Smith, Jonathan, *The Crusades: A Short History*, Yale University Press, New Haven and London, 1987

Rixford, Mrs. (Oscar Herbert) Elizabeth M. Leach, *Families Directly Descended from All the Royal Families in Europe (495 to 1932) and Mayflower Descendants*, originally published Burlington, Vermont, 1932, reprinted for Clearfield by Genealogical Publishing Co., Inc., Baltimore, MD, 1992

Roberts, Gary Boyd, *Ancestors of American Presidents*, 1989

Roll, Winifred, *Mary I: The History of an Unhappy Tudor Queen*, Prentice-Hall, Inc. Englewood Cliffs, New Jersey, 1980

Ross, Charles, *Edward IV*, Eyre Methuem, London, 1974

Ross, Charles, Ed., *Patronage, Pedigree and Power in Later Medieval England*, Alan Sutton, Rowman & Littlefield, 1979

Ross, Josephine, *The Monarchy of Britain*, William Morrow and Company, Inc., NY, 1982

Routh, E. M. G. *Lady Margaret*, 1924

Rowle, John, *Charles the First*, Little, Brown, and Co., Boston, 1975

Sanford, John L., Townsend, Meredith, *Governing Families of England*, Vol I, Books for Libraries Press, Freeport, NY, 1972

Scarisbrick, J. J., *Henry VIII*, University of California Press, Berkeley & Los Angeles, 1968

Bibliography and References

The Spear and the Spindle:
Ancestors of Sir Francis Bryan (d. 1550)
Bryan, Bourchier, Bohun, FitzAlan, and Others

Scofield, Cora L., *The Life and Reign of Edward the Fourth*, Vols. I, II, Frank Cass & Co., Ltd, 1967

Seton, Monsignor, *An Old Family or the Setons of Scotland and America*, Brentano's, NY, 1899

Seward, Desmond, *Eleanor of Aquitaine: The Mother Queen*, Dorset Press, NY, 1978

Seymour, William, *Sovereign Legacy*, Doubleday & Co., Inc., Garden City, NY, 1980

Sharp, Sir Cuthbert, Ed., *The 1569 Rebellion: The Rising in the North*, 1840 Shotton, 1975

Slocombe, George, *William the Conqueror*, GP Putnam's Sons, NY, 1961

Smallwood, Marilu Burch, Compiler, *Related Royal Families*, pub. by author, Storter Printing Co., Gainesville, Fla, 1966

Smith, George, Founder, *Dictionary of National Biography*, Oxford University Press

Smith, Lacey Baldwin, *The Realm of England 1399-1688*

Smith, Lacey Baldwin, *A Tudor Tragedy: The Life and Times of Catherine Howard*, The Reprint Society, London, 1961

Sorley, Janetta C., *King's Daughters*, Cambridge at the University Press, 1937

Spraker, Hazel Atterbury, Comp., *The Boone Family: A Genealogical History of the Descendants of George and Mary Boone who came to America in 1717*, Genealogical Publishing Co., Inc., Baltimore, MD, 1977 (also published by The Tuttle Company, Publishers, Rutland, Vermont, 1922)

St Clare Byrne, Muriel, Ed., *The Lisle Letters*, Penguin Books, 1985

St. Aubyn, Giles, *The Year of Three Kings 1483*, Collins, 8 Grafton St., London W1, 1983

Starkey, David *The Reign of Henry VIII: Personalities and Politics*, Franklin Watts, NY, 1986

Storey, R. L., *End of the House of Lancaster*, Stein and Day, New York, 1967

Strickland, Agnes, *Lives of the Queens of England*, London, 1840-1848

Stringer, K. J., *Earl David of Huntingdon 1152-1219*, Edinburgh University Press, 1985

Stuart, Roderick W., *Royalty for Commoners*, Genealogical Publishing Co., Inc., Baltimore, MD, 1992

Stubbs, W., *The Early Plantagenets*, Scribner, Armstront & Co., New York, 1876

Tey, Josephine, *The Daughter of Time*, The MacMillan Company, New York, 1952

Trease, Geoffrey, *The Seven Queens of England*, The Vanguard Press, Inc., NY 1953

Tuchman, Barbara, *A Distant Mirror: The Calamitous 14th Century*, Alfred A. Knopf, NY, 1978

Turton, Lt.-Col. W. H. Turton, D.S.O., *The Plantagenet Ancestry*, originally published London, 1928, reprinted by Genealogical Publishing Co., Inc., Baltimore, MD, 1993

Unstead, R. J., *See Inside a Castle*, Kingfisher Books, London, 1986

Virgoe, Roger, ed., *Private Life in the Fifteenth Century: Illustrated Letters of the Paston Family*, Weidenfeld & Nicolson, NY, 1989

Warnicke, Retha M., *The Rise and Fall of Anne Boleyn*, Cambridge University Press, Cambridge/NY/Melbourne, 1989

Weis, Frederick Lewis, *Ancestral Roots of Sixty Colonists*, Genealogical Publishing Co., Inc., Baltimore, MD, 1976

The Spear and the Spindle:
Ancestors of Sir Francis Bryan (d. 1550)
Bryan, Bourchier, Bohun, FitzAlan, and Others   Bibliography and References

Weis, Frederick Lewis, *Ancestral Roots of Sixty Colonists Who Came to New England between 1623 and 1650*—6th ed., Genealogical Publishing Co., Inc., Baltimore, MD, 1990

White, Geoffrey H., *The Complete Peerage*, Vol XI, The St Catherine Press, London, 1949

Whitelock, Dorothy, Ed., *The Anglo-Saxon Chronicle*, Rutgers University Press, New Brunswick, NJ, 1961

Whitfield, Emma Morehead, *Whitfield, Bryan, Smith, and Related Families*, 2 vols, Westminster, MD, 1948-50

Wilcox, William B., *The Age of Aristocracy 1688-1830*

Williams, Daniel, Ed., *England in the Fifteenth Century*, The Boydell Press, Suffolk, NH, USA, 1987

Williams, Neville, *Henry VIII and His Court*, The MacMillan Company, NY, 1971

Williamson, David, *Debrett's Kings and Queens of Europe*, Salem House Publishers, Mass., 1988

Williamson, David, *Debrett's Kings and Queens of Britain*, Webb & Bower, Ltd, Devon, London, 1986

Wilson, Derek, *The Tower*, Charles Scribner's Sons, NY, 1979

Wilson, Derek, *The Tower of London*, Constable/Dorset, 1978

Wilson, Violet A., *Queen Elizabeth's Maids of Honour*, John Lane The Bodley Head Limited, London, 1922

Wilson, Violet A., *Queen Elizabeth's Maids of Honor and Ladies of Privy Chamber*, John Lane The Bodley Head Limited, London, 1922

Wise, Terence, *1066: Year of Destiny*, Osprey Publishing Limited, London, 1979

Wurts, John S., *Magna Charta* - Parts I-VII, Brookfield Publishing Co., Philadelphia, Pa, 1945